abc 123

Toronto

Aaron Shutway

must SEES

gswim.chapman@googlemail.com

Editorial Director	Cynthia Clayton Ochterbeck
Editor	Jonathan P. Gilbert
Contributing Writers	Ilona Kauremszky, Anne Dimon, Gwen Cannon
Production Manager	Natasha George
Cartography	Peter Wrenn
Photo Editors	Lydia Strong, Allison M. Simpson
Cover Design	Paris Venise Design — Paris, 17e
Printing and Binding	Himmer AG

Contact us:

Michelin Maps and Guides, One Parkway South, Greenville, SC 29615 USA
www.michelintravel.com
email: michelinguides@us.michelin.com

Special Sales:

For information regarding bulk sales, customized editions and premium sales,
please contact our Customer Service Departments:

USA – 800-423-6277   **Canada** – 800-361-8236

Michelin Apa Publications Ltd
A joint venture between Michelin and Langenscheidt

No part of this publication may be reproduced in any form
without the prior permission of the publisher.

© 2008 Michelin Apa Publications Ltd
ISBN 978-1-906261-32-0

Printed and bound in Germany

Note to the reader:

While every effort is made to ensure that all information printed in this guide is correct
and up-to-date, Michelin Apa Publications Ltd. accepts no liability for any direct, indirect or
consequential losses howsoever caused so far as such can be excluded by law.

Admission prices listed for sights in this guide are for a single adult, unless otherwise
specified.

Welcome to Toronto

Table of Contents

Table of Contents

THE MICHELIN STARS

For more than 75 years, travelers have used the Michelin stars to take the guesswork out of planning a trip. Our star-rating system helps you make the best decision on where to go, what to do, and what to see. A three-star rating means it's one of the "absolutelys"; two stars means it's one of the "should sees"; and one star says it's one of the "sees"—a must if you have the time.

★★★ Absolutely Must See
★★ Really Must See
★ Must See

Three-Star Sights ★★★

CN Tower
Toronto Zoo
Niagara Falls
Ontario Science Centre
Royal Ontario Museum

Two-Star Sights ★★

Art Gallery of Ontario
Bata Shoe Museum
Black Creek Pioneer Village
Casa Loma
Gardiner Museum of Ceramic Art
Harbourfront Centre
McMichael Canadian Art Collection
Niagara-on-the-Lake
Ontario Place
Oshawa
Parkwood Estate
Roy Thomson Hall
Rogers Centre
Toronto-Dominion Centre
Toronto Islands

One-Star Sights ★

African Lion Safari
Campbell House
Canadian Automotive Museum
City Hall
The Distillery Historic District
Dundurn Castle
Eaton Centre
Elgin and Winter Garden Theatre
Fairmont Royal York
First Post Office
Fort George
Fort York
Hamilton
Hockey Hall of Fame
Mackenzie House
Museum of Steam and Technology
Niagara Parks Botanical Gardens
Old City Hall
Old Town Toronto
Ontario Parliament
Osgoode Hall
Queen's Park
Spadina House and Museum
Spencer Clark Collection of Historic Architecture
Toronto Reference Library
Union Station
Wasaga Beach
Yorkville

January

Metro Home Show
Georgia International
Convention Centre   www.dmgworldmedia.com
Toronto International Boat Show
Direct Energy Centre,   416-203-3934
Exhibition Place   www.torontoboatshow.com
Toronto Winterfest
Nathan Phillips Square,
and Mel Lastman Square   www.city.toronto.on.ca

February

International Auto Show
Metro Toronto   905-940-2800
Convention Centre   www.autoshow.ca
Outdoor Adventure Sport Show   905-677-6131
International Centre   www.internationalcentre.com
Spring Fishing Show   416-764-1789
International Centre   www.springfishingshow.com

March

Canada Blooms:
The Flower and Garden Show
Metro Toronto   416-447-8655
Convention Centre   www.CanadaBlooms.com
One of a Kind Spring Canadian
Craft Show and Sale
The Merchandise Mart,   312-527-4141
8th Floor, Chicago   www.oneofakindshow.com
Performance World Custom Car Show   416-229-9919
International Centre   performanceworldcarshow.com
St. Patrick's Day Parade
Downtown   www.topatrick.com
Toronto Sportsmen's Show
Direst Energy Centre,
Exhibition Place   www.sportsmensshows.com

April

Creative Sewing & Needlework Festival 800.291.2030
International Centre (Apr & Oct)   www.csnf.com
National Home Show
Direcy Energy Centre,   416-385-1880
Exhibition Place   www.nationalhomeshow.com

June

Gay & Lesbian Pride Day Parade
Yonge St. between   416 927 7433
Dundas & Bloor Sts.   www.pridetoronto.com
Metro Toronto International Caravan 416-856-6482
Various locations   www.caravan-org.com
Toronto Downtown Jazz Festival
Nathan Phillips Square &   416-928-2033
various other locations   www.torontojazz.com

Toronto International Dragon
Boat Race Festival   416-595-0313
Toronto Islands   www.dragonboats.com

July

Beaches International Jazz Festival   416-698-2152
Queen St. E.   www.beachesjazz.com

Celebrate Toronto Street Festival
www.city.toronto.on.ca   416-395-0490
Yonge & Bloor Sts. and other major downtown intersections

Grand Prix of Toronto
Exhibition Grounds,   416.588.7223
Exhibition Place   www.grandprixtoronto.com

Outdoor Art Exhibition   416-408-2754
Nathan Phillips Square   www.torontooutdoorart.org

Toronto International Carnival/Caribana
Various locations   www.torontocarnival.com

August

Canadian National Exhibition (CNE)   416-393-6300
Exhibition Place   www.theex.com

September

International Home Show   416-512-1305
International Centre   www.home-show.net

Toronto International Film Festival
Various locations downtown   www.bell.ca/filmfest

October

Fall Home Show   416-385-1880
Georgia International
Convention Centre   www.dmgworldmedia.com

International Festival of Authors   416-973-3000
Harbourfront Centre   www.readings.org

Toronto Marathon
Begins at Mel Lastman Square,   416-972-1062
Yonge St. near Hollywood Ave.   www.runtoronto.com

November

The Royal Agricultural Winter Fair
Direst Energy Centre,   416-263-3400
Exhibition Place   www.royalfair.org

December

Cavalcade of Lights   416-395-0490
Nathan Phillips Square   www.city.toronto.on.ca

New Year's Eve   416-395-0490
City Hall   www.city.toronto.on.ca

Canadian Craft Show and Sale
The Merchandise Mart,   312-527-4141
8th Floor, Chicago   www.oneofakindshow.com

Santa Claus Parade
Begins on Bloor St.   www.thesantaclausparade.com

Must Know: Practical Information

WHEN TO GO

The main tourist season for most of Canada, including Toronto, begins the last weekend in May (Victoria Day) and lasts until the first weekend in September (Labour Day). Many attractions extend the season to the Thanksgiving weekend (second Monday in October).

From mid-April to mid-May, visitors can usually enjoy comfortable daytime temperatures but expect chilly nights. July and August are hot and often humid with temperatures ranging from 22°–32°C/70°–90°F. Many regions outside Toronto (cottage country and the southern regions along the Canada/US border) offer spectacular displays of fall colors from mid-September until mid-October. For the sports enthusiast, the bracing Canadian winter (mid-Nov–mid-Mar) offers excellent opportunities for downhill and cross-country skiing.

Average Seasonal Temperatures in Toronto

	Jan	Apr	July	Oct
Avg. High	-1°C / 30°F	11°C / 52°F	26°C / 79°F	14°C / 57°F
Avg. Low	-7°C / 19°F	4°C / 39°F	18°C / 64°F	7°C / 45°F

PLANNING YOUR TRIP

Before you go, contact the following tourist organizations in and around the Toronto area for information about sightseeing, accommodations, recreation and annual events.

Toronto Convention & Visitors Association

207 Queen's Quay W., Toronto, Ontario, M5J 1A7 Canada
416-203-2600; www.torontotourism.com

Ontario Tourism

Hearst Block, 900 Bay St., 4th floor
Toronto, Ontario, M7A 2E1 Canada
416-314-7550; www.ontariotravel.net

City of Toronto

Toronto City Hall 100 Queen St. W.,
Toronto, Ontario, M5H 2N2 Canada
416-395-6457; www.toronto.ca

Toronto Special Events

Toronto City Hall, East Tower
100 Queen St. W., 9th floor
Toronto, Ontario, M5H 2N2 Canada
416-395-0490; www.toronto.ca/special_events

Toronto Tourism

207 Queen's Quay W., 5th floor
Queen's Quay Terminal
Toronto, Ontario, M5J 1A7 Canada

Toronto Online
In addition to the official Toronto Tourism Web site above, try this one for useful visitor information:
www.toronto.com

Ontario Travel Information Centre

> 20 Dundas St. W, Atrium on Bay
> Toronto, Ontario, M5G 2C2 Canada

GETTING THERE

By Air – Pearson International Airport (YYZ) is located 25km/15mi west of downtown *(416-247-7678 or 866-207-1690; www.gtaa.ca)*. Air Canada *888-247-2262; www.aircanada.com)* connects to regions throughout the province. Taxi service to downtown costs $55. Airport shuttle: Airport Express Aeroport *($17; 905-564-3232; www.torontoairportexpress.com)*. Major car rental agencies are located at the airport.

Travellers pay an **Airport Improvement Fee**, which is shown separately on the purchased ticket *(departing passengers pay $20; connecting passengers pay $8)*.

By Train – Canada's national passenger service, VIA rail operates out of Union Station in downtown Toronto. In Canada, consult the telephone directory for the nearest office *(from the US, call 800-561-3949; www.viarail.ca)*.

Union Station is the hub for the TTC subway *(www.ttc.com)* and the Go-Transit systems *(www.gotransit.com)*. Go-Transit serves an 8,000sq km area radiating from downtown to Hamilton and Guelph in the west; Orangeville, Barrie and Beaverton to the north; and Port Perry, Oshawa and Newcastle to the east.

By Bus – The city's main bus terminal *(202-289-5154)* is located at 610 Bay St. The major bus line is Greyhound *(416-367-8747; www.greyhound.ca)*.

By Car – Toronto is situated on the north shore of Lake Ontario and is accessible by Highway 401 (east-west), the Don Valley Parkway (north-south), Lakeshore Boulevard (east-west) and the Gardiner Expressway (east-west).

GETTING AROUND

The Grid – Downtown city streets are laid out in a grid. Main streets (University, Bay, Yonge, Jarvis & Sherbourne) run north-south, while others (King, Queen, Dundas, College/Carlton, Wellesley & Bloor) run east-west. Yonge Street is the dividing line between the east and west sides of the city. Lake Ontario lies to the south. Toronto is a good walking city, and once you understand the grid, finding a street number is relatively easy if you know the closest main intersection *(for details on finding an address, see back cover flap)*.

By Car – Toronto's downtown streets can get very congested, especially during rush hours *(weekdays 7am–9am & 4:30pm–6pm)*. Note that many downtown

---

In The News

The city's leading daily newspaper is the Toronto Star *(www.thestar.ca)*; it includes a section on the Greater Toronto Area. The Star's Thursday "What's On" section carries an extensive list of what's happening around the city in terms of entertainment; and the Travel section on Saturday offers ideas for day trips.

Other newspapers include the *Toronto Sun (www.torontosun.com)*; the *Globe & Mail (www.globeandmail.com)* and the *National Post (www.nationalpost.com)*. The latter two provide more of a national focus.

streets are also one-way. The use of seat belts is mandatory. Parking spaces on downtown streets are limited and parking regulations are strictly enforced. Some metered parking is available on the street, and parking garages are plentiful. Posted rush-hour restrictions generally prohibit parking and stopping during rush hours *(times can vary)*.

Car Rental Company	Reservations	Internet
Avis	800-331-1212	www.avis.com
Budget	800-527-0700	www.drivebudget.com
Enterprise	800-325-8007	www.enterprise.com
Hertz	800-654-3131	www.hertz.com
National	800-227-7368	www.nationalcar.com
Thrifty	800-331-4200	www.thrifty.com

Parking – Parking signs are color-coded: green-and-white signs indicate hours when parking is allowed; red-and-white signs indicate hours when it isn't. Stopping during restricted times could result in your vehicle being towed.

Public Transportation

TTC – The Toronto Transit Commission operates an extensive public transportation system of buses, streetcars and subway lines. Hours of operation: Mon–Sat 6am–1:30am, Sun 9am–1:30am. Adult fare is $2.75 one-way for unlimited travel with no stopovers *(exact fare required; drivers do not sell tickets)*. A Day Pass, good for unlimited one-day travel, is $9. Family Holiday Passes *($9)* are good for unlimited one-day travel on weekends and holidays for a family consisting of two adults and up to four children. Free transfers between buses & streetcars. For route information, call 416-393-4636 or visit www.ttc.ca.

Important Numbers	
Emergency (Police, Ambulance, Fire Department, 24hrs)	911
Police (non-emergency)	416-808-2222
Poison Information	416-813-5900
Crime Stoppers	800-222-8477
Dental Emergency Service (8am–midnight)	416-485-7121
24-hour Pharmacy – Shoppers Drug Mart	
3089 Duffering St. at Lawrence St.	416-787-0238
2345 Yonge St. at Eglinton St.	416-487-5411
700 Bay St. at Gerard St.	416-979-2424
Weather	416-661-0123

Taxis – Numerous taxi companies operate in the city under the licensing supervision of the Taxi Industry Unit *(416-392-3082)*. When the "Taxi" sign on the roof of the cab is lit, the vehicle is for hire. The meter starts at $3 and increases by 25¢ for every .190km (except airport transportation, which may be charged at a set rate).

TELEPHONES

Area Codes: 416 and 647
Area codes must now be used in the Toronto area.

TIPS FOR SPECIAL VISITORS

Disabled Travellers – All public buildings and many attractions, restaurants and hotels provide wheelchair access. Disabled parking is provided and the law is strictly enforced. Many national and provincial parks have restrooms, trails and other facilities for the disabled *(for details, call 888-773-8888 or visit www. parkscanada.gc.ca)*. Additional information is available from Easter Seals Canada *(90 Eglinton Ave. E., Suite 511, Toronto, Ontario M4P 2Y3 Canada; 416-932-8382; www.easterseals.ca)*.

For Via Rail Special Needs Services call 800-268-9503/TDD *(or 888-842-7245; www.viarail.ca)*. For information about bus travel, contact Greyhound Canada *(800-661-8747 or 800-345-3109/TDD; www.greyhound.ca)*.

Senior Citizens – Many attractions, hotels, restaurants, entertainment venues and public transportation systems offer discounts to visitors age 65 or older (proof of age may be required). Canada's national parks usually offer discount fees for seniors. For more information, contact the Canadian Association for the 50 Plus *(416-363-8748 or 800-363-9736; www.carp.ca)*.

INTERNATIONAL VISITORS

In addition to local tourism offices, visitors may obtain information from the nearest Canadian embassy or consulate in their country of residence. Many foreign countries maintain consulates in Toronto. For further information on all Canadian embassies and consulates abroad, visit the Web site of the Canadian Department of Foreign Affairs and International Trade: *www.dfait-maeci.gc.ca*.

Entry Requirements – Citizens of the US visiting Canada need proof of citizenship (a valid passport, or a driver's license together with a birth certificate or a voter's registration card). All other visitors to Canada must have a valid passport and, in some cases, a visa. No vaccinations are necessary. For entry into Canada via the US, all persons other than US citizens or legal residents are required to present a valid passport. Check with the Canadian embassy or consulate in your home country about entry regulations and proper travel documents.

Canada Customs – Non-residents may import personal baggage temporarily without payment of duties. All prescription drugs should be clearly labeled and for personal use only; visitors should carry a copy of the prescription. For details, call the Canada Border Service Agency *(416-973-8022, Toronto; 800-461-9999)* or write to Canada Revenue Agency Ottawa, Ontario, K1A 0L5 Canada *(www.cbsa.gc.ca)*.

Canada has stringent legislation on **firearms**. For further information, contact the Canadian Firearms Centre *(Canadian Firearms Centre, Ottawa, Ontario K1A 1M6 Canada; 800-731-4000; www.cfc-caf.gc.ca)*.

Money and Currency Exchange – Visitors can exchange currency at downtown banks as well as at Pearson International Airport and hotels. Banks, stores, restaurants and hotels accept travellers' cheques with picture identification.

To report a **lost or stolen credit card**: American Express *(800-528-4800)*; Diners Club *(800-234-6377)*; MasterCard *(800-307-7309)*; or Visa *(800-336-8472)*.

Must Know: Practical Information

Driving in Canada – Visitors bearing valid driver's licenses issued by their country of residence are not required to obtain an International Driver's License. Drivers must carry vehicle registration and/or rental contract, and proof of automobile insurance at all times. Gasoline is sold by the litre. Vehicles in Canada are driven on the right-hand side of the road.

Electricity – Voltage in Canada is 120 volts AC, 60 Hz. Foreign-made appliances may need AC adapters (available at specialty travel and electronics stores) and North American two-prong, flat-blade plugs.

Tipping – It's customary to give a small gift of money—a tip—for services rendered, to waiters (15–20% of bill), porters ($1 per bag), chamber maids at hotels ($1 per day) and cab drivers (15% of fare).

Toronto Taxes

Prices displayed in Canada do not include sales tax. In Toronto (as in the rest of Canada) the Goods & Services Tax (GST) is a 7% tariff that is added to most goods and services. Foreign visitors can apply for a rebate on the GST that is paid on accommodations in Canada and on certain goods purchased in Canada and taken out of the country. Goods consumed in the country are not eligible for rebate. GST rebate forms are available from hotels, gift shops and duty-free shops. Original receipts are required. For more information, check online at: www.canadasalestaxrefunds.com.

Metric System – Canada uses the International System of weights and measures. Weather temperatures are given in Celsius (C°), milk and wine are sold by millilitres and litres, and grocery items are measured in grams. All distances and speed limits are posted in kilometres (to obtain the approximate equivalent in miles, multiply by 0.6). Some examples of metric conversions are:

1 kilometre (km) = 0.62 miles
1 litre (L) = 33.8 fluid ounces = 0.26 gallons

1 metre (m) = 3.28 feet
1 US quart = 32 fluid ounces

Temperature Equivalents

Degrees Fahrenheit	95°	86°	77°	68°	59°	50°	41°	32°	23°	14°
Degrees Celsius	35°	30°	25°	20°	15°	10°	5°	0°	-5°	-10°

ACCOMMODATIONS

For a list of specific suggested accommodations, see Must Stay.

Tourism Toronto - 416-203-2500 or 800-363-1990; www.tourismtoronto.com.
Bed & Breakfast Homes of Toronto - 416-363-6362; www.bbht.ca.
Bed & Breakfast Metropolitan Registry of Toronto - 416-964-2566.

Campgrounds & Hostels – Glen Rouge Campground in Rouge Park *(416-338-2267)*. **Ontario Parks** *(888-668-7275; www.ontarioparks.com)*. Hostels are a great choice for budget travellers. Most have both private rooms and dormitories, as well as kitchens and laundry facilities. **Global Village Backpackers** *(460 King St. W.; 416-703-8540; www.globalbackpackers.com)*, charges between $25 and $30/night and is open year-round. Hostelling International also maintains a facility in Toronto *(76 Church St.; 416-971-4440 or 877-848-8738; www.hihostels.ca)*.

Major hotel and motel chains with locations in Toronto

Property	Phone	Web site
Best Western	800-528-1234	www.bestwestern.com
Choice Hotels	877-316-9951	www.choicehotels.com
Days Inn	800-325-2525	www.daysinn.com
Delta Hotels	800-268-1133	www.deltahotels.com
Fairmont	800-441-1414	www.fairmont.com
Four Seasons	800-332-3442	www.fourseasons.com
Hilton	800-221-2424	www.hilton.com
Holiday Inn	800-465-4329	www.holiday-inn.com
Marriott	800-847-5075	www.marriott.com
Novotel	800-221-4542	www.novotel.com
Radisson Inn	800-333-3333	www.radisson.com
Ramada Inn	800-854-7854	www.ramadainn.com
Sheraton	800-325-3535	www.sheraton.com
Westin	800-228-3000	www.westin.com

SPECTATOR SPORTS

Here's a list of Toronto's major professional sports teams. For tickets to games of all teams listed below, call Ticketmaster *(416-872-5000)*.

Sport/Team	Season	Venue	Phone	Web site
Baseball/Toronto Blue Jays (AL)	Apr–Oct	SkyDome	416-341-1111	www.bluejays.ca
Football/Toronto Argonauts (CFL)	mid-Jun–Nov	SkyDome	416-489-2745	www.argonauts.on.ca
Basketball/Toronto Raptors (NBA)	Nov–Apr	Air Canada Centre	416-366-3865	www.raptors.com
Hockey/Toronto Maple Leafs (NHL)	Oct–Apr	Air Canada Centre	416-815-5500	www.torontomapleleafs.com

Toronto

From Good to Great: Toronto

Dynamic, cosmopolitan, stimulating—that's Toronto. The cultural and financial heart of the country, Toronto is Canada's largest metropolis, and the fifth-largest city in North America, with a metropolitan area that's home to 4.5 million people. This vibrant multicultural city—the provincial capital of Ontario—offers colourful neighbourhoods, world-class museums and performing arts, architectural treasures, professional sports teams, great shopping and fine cuisine. All this, and an enviable location on Lake Ontario that makes for some awesome recreational opportunities.

Before 1600, the native Huron and Petun peoples abandoned their lands on the north shore to the warring Iroquois Confederacy. The Iroquois occupied the vacated territory to strengthen their fur trade, only to be evicted themselves by French traders, to whom the "Toronto Passage" of trails and canoe routes between lakes Huron and Ontario was well known.

French fur traders met native and English traders at a bartering post on the Humber River on the site of present-day Toronto (the city's name is a Huron word for "meeting place"). To curb competition, the French began constructing forts around Lake Ontario in 1720. Remains of one of these forts—Fort Rouillé—have been found in Toronto's Exhibition Grounds. To prevent the British from using it, the French destroyed the fort in 1759 during the Seven Years' War, the conflict that signalled the end of French presence in the area.

The new British rulers first ignored the site, but in 1787, the governor of British North America arranged to buy land from the Mississaugas, who had occupied it after the Iroquois. Loyalists fleeing the US had also settled along the lake; their demands for English law led to the formation of Upper Canada (now Ontario) in 1791.

Colonel John Graves Simcoe, lieutenant-governor of the new territory, chose Toronto as the temporary capital because of its good harbour and distance from the American border. Called York in honor of the soldier-son of King George III, the new outpost grew slowly. In 1813 the town was jolted by an American fleet that set fire to the legisla-

Mackenzie's Rebellion

In the 1830s a group of wealthy men with strong British ties dominated the government of York—and Upper Canada. William Lyon Mackenzie, an outspoken Scot, attacked this "Family Compact" in his newspaper. He was elected to the legislative assembly, led the radical wing of the Reform Party and served as Toronto's first mayor (the City was incorporated in 1834). When he reassumed his seat in the legislature, the governor dissolved the assembly.

Getting no satisfaction from British Parliament, Mackenzie turned to armed rebellion in 1837, but the revolt collapsed, and Mackenzie fled to the US. Although two of Mackenzie's men were hanged, the revolt was effective in that the British Parliament ultimately granted "responsible government" to the Canadian colonies. The united Province of Canada was created, and Mackenzie was eventually allowed to return.

tive and other buildings. In retaliation, the British burned part of Washington, DC, the capital of the US, in 1814.

Mackenzie's revolt *(see sidebar, p 19)* bred among Toronto's residents an enduring hatred of violence and a resulting support for the government. As a major manufacturing centre, the city had become immensely wealthy by the end of the 19C. Prosperous financiers, industrialists and merchants were united in their belief that intemperance was a fundamental social problem. Indeed, the city, christened "Toronto the Good," had gained a reputation for its Anglo-Saxon morality (read stuffiness).

As late as 1941, Toronto was 80 percent Anglo-Saxon, but since World War II, the city has opened its doors to immigrants from around the world. Today Italians, Germans, Ukrainians, Dutch, Poles, Scandinavians, Portuguese, East Indians, Chinese, West Indians and other nationalities have made their home here, giving Toronto a stimulating mix of cultures, which is reflected in the city's diverse neighbourhoods and ethnic restaurants.

The last 30 years have seen the Toronto skyline transformed. Shining glass-fronted skyscrapers and "spacescraper" CN Tower overshadow the once-dominant Royal York Hotel and the Canadian Imperial Bank of Commerce. Rapid development has been highly controversial, however. Citizen-action groups formed to halt destruction of residential areas for proposed freeways and high rises. The city was the first in North America to adopt a tiered system of metropolitan government to solve the problems caused by 19C municipal boundaries.

In 1998 Toronto became a megacity when the six municipalities that make up Greater Toronto were combined. Comfortable in the recent past to sit on its laurels, Toronto is now taking a hard look at its future. Highlights include the creation of new neighbourhoods like the Distillery Historic District in the city's core; the upgrading of local colleges and universities; major expansion of cultural institutions, namely the Royal Ontario Museum, the Art Gallery of Ontario and the Four Seasons Centre for the Performing Arts; as well as revitalization plans for Union Station, the city's transportation hub.

Meanwhile, the completion of such projects as Dundas Square, with its high-tech signage rivalling that of New York City's Times Square, and the $100 million entertainment and retail complex Metropolis have pumped new blood into downtown. Come experience for yourself all the reasons why so many people now call Toronto "great."

You know you're in Toronto when you spot the space-needlelike structure of CN Tower. Along with the Rogers Centre and the Parliament Buildings, these landmarks define the city's skyline. Some of Toronto's 19C icons, like Old City Hall, Union Station and Osgoode Hall are shorter, but they're still massive enough to represent the city's fortitude and staying power.

CN Tower★★★

Front & John Sts. (take Skywalk from Union Station). 416-868-6937. www.cntower.ca. Open Jun–Oct daily 9am–10:30pm. Rest of the year daily 9am–10pm (Fri & Sat until 11pm); call for holiday hours. Closed Dec 25. $32.

This needle-nosed cloud tickler reaches over 553m/1,815ft in height. The **views**★★★ from its observation decks are so spectacular, it's no wonder that for over 30 years it held the title as the world's tallest free-standing structure until it was recently surpassed by the Burj Dubai in Dubai.

The $63 million structure was built in the 1970s by Canadian National Railways as a telecommunications tower. Its powerful antenna services FM radio and television stations, whose transmitters line the mast. At the base of the tower you can interact with computers and watch video presentations. But the real rush is the glass elevator ride in which you arrive to the "turban," 346m/1,135ft high in a lightning 58 seconds. This **lookout level** is a good place

to orient yourself to Toronto for views of the city and the lake.

One floor below, the fearless can stand (or sit) on the **glass floor**—a section of thick glass with dizzying views 342m/1,122ft straight down. If heights don't bother you, take the elevator 33 storeys higher to **Skypod**, a flying-saucer-shaped ring 447m/1,467ft above the ground. Here, you'll be higher than the planes from nearby Toronto Island Airport! Still not dizzy? Then you're good-to-go to the tower's **360 Restaurant**, the world's highest revolving restaurant, where the view can't be topped *(see Must Eat)*.

How Big Is It?
- **Height:** 553m/1,815ft to the top of the antenna
- **Weight:** 117,910 metric tonnes (130,000 tons), or the equivalent of 23,214 large elephants
- **Strength:** The tower sways a little; in winds of 193km/hr (120mph) with 200mph gusts, the tower sphere moves .5m/19in from the centre.
- **Cost:** $63 million (over $250 million in today's dollars)

Roy Thomson Hall★★

60 Simcoe St. 416-872-4255. www.roythomson.com. Other than performances, visit is by guided tour only, call for hours. Reservations required. $7.

From the street, this concert hall at the corner of King and Simcoe looks like a giant, upside-down salad bowl.

The hall was named for Canadian newspaper magnate Roy Thomson, and designed by architect Arthur Erickson to bring out the best in sound. A thick circular passageway with entry doors at intervals creates a "sound lock" that insulates the performance area.

Beginning with the new millennium, the hall underwent a two-year reengineering to incorporate the latest in sound technology. Now there's new maple flooring, a new stage door and new acoustical canopies.

Since 1982 the concert hall has been the home of the Toronto Symphony. Today, Roy Thomson Hall caters to a variety of musical tastes, presenting jazz, classical, world music, dance concerts—and even stand-up comedy. The hall has its own music store, one that's especially strong in classical offerings. If you can't attend a performance, take a tour of the facility for a behind-the-scenes look.

Hall Of Stars
Singers **Anne Murray** and **Gordon Lightfoot**, dancer **Karen Kain**, the Canadian Opera Company, and the Canadian Brass all performed at the hall's opening.
Other outstanding musicians who have played here include **Isaac Stern**, **Itzhak Perlman**, **Pinchas Zuckerman**, **Jean-Pierre Rampal** and **Yo-Yo Ma**.
Conductors **Leonard Bernstein** and **Seiji Ozawa** have raised their batons here.

Rogers Centre★★

One Blue Jays Way (take the Skywalk from Union Station). 416-341-2770. www.rogerscentre.com. Open daily for 1hr guided tour; call for schedule. $13.50.

This huge stadium can hold a lot of birds—Toronto Blue Jays, that is. Home to the two-time World Series champions, the Toronto Blue Jays Major League baseball team, as well as rock concerts, conventions and trade shows, the Rogers Centre sits on railway land west of CN Tower.

Big-name entertainers like Phil Collins, Madonna, Van Halen and Aerosmith have all performed here; and football greats Doug Flutie and Mike Vanderjagt have played on the arena's field with the Toronto Argonauts. In fact, the field is so flexible, it can be configured for baseball, football, basketball, tennis or track events (changing the field from baseball to football requires 8 to 10 hours). Seating can be arranged for an audience of 10,000 or a crowd of 55,000. But the best thing about Rogers Centre is its retractable roof—all 3 ha/8 acres of it. Events can be held outdoors without getting rained out. In only 20 minutes, the panels close by the mere push of a button. It's all computer-controlled.

The Rogers Centre also contains the 348-room Renaissance Toronto Hotel with each room overlooking the playing field. There's also a 150-seat cinema, several restaurants and underground parking for 575 vehicles. The stadium was completed in 1989 for over $570 million, and by 1993 Roger Centre had received its 25 millionth visitor. As you arrive at the Front Street entrance, look up to see the painted fibreglass sculptures of stadium "fans" by Michael Snow. Once inside, you can take a 45-minute tour that includes the Press Box, and the Hall of Fame. Depending upon scheduled events, you might even get to actually go on the field.

> **Up On The Roof**
> **Width:** At its widest, the roof measures 205m/673ft.
> **Height:** At its centre, 91m/299ft—tall enough to hold a 31-storey building.
> **Weight:** 12,122 metric tonnes/11,000 tons—as much as 3,732 cars
> **Size:** 3.2 hectares/8 acres
> **Speed:** The roof moves 21m/69ft per minute; it can open (or close) in 20 minutes.

Toronto-Dominion Centre★★

66 Wellington St. W. 416-869-1144. www.tdcentre.com Open year-round daily 6am–7pm. Businesses closed major holidays.

The locals call it T-D Centre. These ebony-colored towers cover an entire city block, bounded by York, King, Wellington and Bay streets. The Toronto Dominion Bank Tower, which opened in 1967, was the first skyscraper in the current financial district. Initially only three buildings and now there are six of these spare black-glass and steel towers, designed in the International style by famous 20C architect Mies van der Rohe. A seventh tower, built of red granite *(95 Wellington St. W.)* was purchased by the centre in 1987.

Total rentable area of the office towers is 399,500sq m/4,300,000sq ft. Currently, over 100 tenants in banking, marketing, and other services are based here. At the Concourse level, over 70 retail stores specialize in ladies' and men's fashions, footwear, and other merchandise. On the 54th floor of the T-D Bank Tower, the famed restaurant Canoe *(see Must Eat)*, welcomes diners with great food and grand city views. The lower level has a bustling fast-food court.

Inside the tower at 79 Wellington Street West, there's a **Gallery of Inuit Art** *(on the ground level)*, which showcases the Bank's formidable collection; there's no fee, and you can book a personalized guided tour if you like.

Outside on the grounds west of the Toronto-Dominion Bank Tower sit seven life-sized **bronze cows**. Artist Joe Fafard wanted city folks to remember the rural countryside that used to be here and how they depended upon the pastures. Each immoveable bovine weighs 544 kilograms/1,200 pounds and is nearly 3m/9.8ft long.

The Towers:

Toronto Dominion Bank Tower (TD) – *66 Wellington St. W*. This 56-storey tower houses the offices of Toronto Dominion Bank; on the 54th floor, Canoe restaurant includes an observation deck.

TD Banking Pavilion – This one-storey clear-span building (with no columns) is annexed to the T-D Tower.

Ernst & Young Tower – *222 Bay St*. The 32-storey tower encloses within its base the former Art Deco Stock Exchange Building (1937), and serves as the Canadian headquarters of Ernst & Young, a global business-services company.

79 Wellington Street West – On the south side of Wellington, this 39-floor tower is mostly occupied by business tenants specializing in legal and financial services. At the top level, there's a fitness centre complete with a running track and swimming pool.

Canadian Pacific Tower – Closest to York Street, this 33-storey structure contains the eastern regional executive offices for the Fairmont Hotels firm.

95 Wellington Street West – A 22-floor high rise occupied by companies specializing in legal, investment, real estate, mining and financial services.

Royal Trust Tower – Closer to King Street, this 43-storey tower is devoted to financial and banking services. A sit-down restaurant occupies space in the plaza.

Not Just "Business As Usual"

Though its primary function is business, the T-D Centre plays host to a number of community activities that attract participants and spectators alike. It's the outdoor setting for events like the popular **Warmth Ball Hockey Challenge** every year in June, when three rinks are created in the centre's courtyard as a stage for games and celebrities. At the **Tennis Festival in the Courtyard,** a regulation-size court is set up here to host junior and celebrity matches as well as a tennis clinic. A "smash cage" is reserved for players who want to practice their serves. Musical performances, such as the Sounds of Toronto Summer concert series, Talent Day for budding musicians, and an improv comedy festival, are regularly held outside on the grounds of T-D Centre.

City Hall★

Nathan Phillips Square, 100 Queen St. W. 416-338-0338. www.toronto.ca. Open year-round Mon–Fri 7:30am–10:30pm, Sat–Sun & holidays 8am–10pm.

You can't miss City Hall. Sitting at the edge of a large pool, two half-moon shaped towers surround a council chamber that resembles a saucer spaceship. When City Hall was completed in 1965, this masterpiece by Finland's Viljo Revell was the symbol of Toronto, and so it remained until the CN Tower was constructed. The big plaza in front of City Hall is Nathan Phillips Square, named for a former mayor. In winter, the pool transforms into an ice rink frequented by crowds of ice-skaters. If you like Henry Moore sculptures, be sure to see his bronze piece, *The Archer*.

Seat Of Power

As it has been since 1834, the City of Toronto is administered by a mayor/councillor form of government. Originally appointed by council, the mayor has been an elected office since 1870, and currently serves three years. The 44 elected city councillors also serve a three-year term. Inside City Hall, these officials organize and carry out their work according to six standing committees: Policy and Finance, Administration, Planning and Transportation, Economic Development and Parks, Community Services and Works Committee. Responsibilities of each Standing Committee are outlined in the Council Procedural By-law. The public is encouraged to participate in the municipal decision-making process.

Old City Hall★

[A] *refers to map on inside front cover. 60 Queen St. W. at Bay St. 416-392-8583. www.city.toronto.on. ca/old_cityhall. Open year−round Mon−Thu 8am−9pm, Fri 8am−5pm.*

Fortunately, Toronto didn't demolish the old city hall when the new one was built. Old City Hall stands near its new cousin on the east side of the square *(60 Queen St. W.)*. It's the building with the extremely tall clock tower, the face of which measures 6m/20ft in diameter. This previous home of the city fathers—from 1899 to 1965—now houses the provincial courts. Toronto native Edward J. Lennox designed the massive building in the ornate Richardsonian Romanesque style. Construction began in 1889 and the building officially opened in 1899, during which time the architect had some fun with the building. Over the front steps you'll see several grostesque faces—thought to be political figures of the time. Look carefully and see "E.J. Lennox, Architect A.D. 1898" spaced under the eaves of all four faces of the building (Lennox left his mark, but probably without official permission). When the hall opened, a number of interesting items were placed in the cornerstone, for posterity's sake *(see sidebar below)*. Step inside Old City Hall to see the fancy patterned-tile floors and the copper-painted capitals topping the marble columns. Peek behind the grand iron staircase to see the large stained-glass window with scenes symbolizing the city's growth.

The Cornerstone's Cache

Coins and printed pieces of historical note were placed in Old City Hall's cornerstone when it was laid in 1891, including copies of five Toronto newspapers *(The Empire, Evening Telegram, Globe, Mail,* and *News and World)*, a map of the city, a copy of the national song "The Maple Leaf Forever," 1891 coins and two- and four-dollar bills. Coins taken from an earlier city hall, including an American dime, were inserted, as well as a scrolled record of the cornerstone ceremony and a list of the city's 1890 by-laws. Made of New Brunswick stone, the cornerstone measured six feet long and weighed about six tons. It was placed at the southwest corner of the clock tower.

Ontario Parliament ★

Queen's Park, north of College St. 416-325-7500. www.ontla.on.ca. Open Victoria Day–Labour Day Mon–Fri 10am–4pm, Sat–Sun & holidays 9am–4pm. Rest of the year Mon–Fri 10am–4pm.

A lot of important decisions about Ontario are made in this impressive sandstone structure in lovely Queen's Park. This is the Ontario Parliament. It's essentially the seat, or centre, of provincial government. The Legislative Building opened back in 1893, but not without a fuss. A design competition was held in 1880 to select the architect, but the winners' bids turned out to be more than the government could pay. So in 1885, one of the contest's judges, American-based Richard Waite awarded himself the six-year, million-dollar project.

Inside, the interior is indeed elegant, particularly the west wing, rebuilt of white Italian marble after a fire in 1909. The walls of the legislative chamber, or House, where the Legislative Assembly meets, are richly finished in mahogany and sycamore panelling. The Speaker of the House, sits in the ornately carved chair backed by a large mahogany Royal Coat of Arms. One of the most interesting items is the 200-year-old mace on the ground floor; it's the ceremonial gold "club" that symbolizes the Speaker's authority, and its presence is required at House proceedings. During the War of 1812, the Americans took the mace when they assaulted York in 1813. Years later, US president Franklin D. Roosevelt returned it.

Government In Action

The public is invited to watch a legislative session from the visitors' galleries. When in session, the House assembles Mon–Thu 1:30pm–6pm and Thu 10am–noon. You can get free passes at the south basement entrance, located to the left of the main doors. Before viewing the session, visitors must check their belongings at the attended coat room.

It's Parliamentary

Here's a basic primer of terms relating to Ontario's Parliament:

Backbencher – A "private member" who is not a minister, parliamentary assistant or leading member of the opposition. Historically, he or she occupied a back bench in the Legislative Chamber.

Bicameral – A legislative body with two houses. For example, the Parliament of Canada has an upper and lower house—the Senate and the House of Commons.

Hansard – The official, verbatim record of the daily proceedings of the House and its committees. Sessions are tape-recorded as well as transcribed.

House – The Legislative Assembly of Ontario, consisting of 103 members, including the Speaker. Also refers to the Legislative Chamber, the room where the Legislative Assembly meets.

Legislative Assembly – The governing body that debates and makes laws. It is sometimes referred to as the legislature, or the house.

Speaker – The Speaker is elected by all the members of the legislature to preside over all meetings of the house in a fair and impartial manner. The Speaker upholds all the rules of procedure and ensures that the business of the house is carried out in an orderly manner.

Source: The Legislative Assembly of Ontario

Osgoode Hall★

130 Queen St. W. 416-947-3300. www.osgoodehall.com
Open year-round Mon–Fri 8:30am–5pm.

Order in the court. One of the oldest surviving structures in Toronto, Osgoode Hall serves as the home of the Supreme Court of Ontario and the Law Society of Upper Canada *(see sidebar)*. In 1829 the Society purchased six acres in what was then pastureland outside the town limits. Completed in 1832, this Neo-classical building originally consisted of only the east wing. The structure, which stands west of Nathan Phillips Square, was named for William Osgoode, the first provincial chief justice (1792–1794).

With some 10 major additions over the years, Osgoode Hall is actually a series of connected structures, containing 20 levels within 6 floors for a total of 19,603sq m/211,000sq ft of labyrinthian corridors. The first of the additions occurred in 1833: two dozen bedrooms were added to the east wing for law students. From 1838 to 1843, troops were quartered in the hall after Mackenzie's Rebellion; needless to say, it had to be upgraded in 1844. The central pavilion and west wing were then added, and the facade and interior were altered. In 1846 the Society agreed to allow the Superior Courts to occupy space at the hall. Twenty-two years later the cast-iron fence that lines the expansive lawns was put up, allegedly to keep cows out. Today the east wing is home to the Benchers, the governing body of the Law Society of Upper Canada. There are also offices for the Society's staff, classrooms and lecture halls.

Legal Beagles

One of the oldest professional bodies in North America, the **Law Society of Upper Canada** was established in 1797. Only the Boston Bar Association predates it. Incorporated in 1822, the Society was created by legislative mandate to set professional standards, take responsibility for educating Ontario's future lawyers and oversee their admission to the practice of law. With a current list of some 32,000 lawyers, the Society provides legal information, referrals, legal aid and other services to its members as well as to the public. Along with provincial government, the Society co-owns Osgoode Hall.

You can take a tour of the interior of Osgoode Hall. But you'll have to be quiet when you're touring, since the court may be in session.

The Courtyard – The dominant feature of the two-tiered, arched courtyard is its lovely stained-glass roof.

Convocation Hall – This space was modeled after the medieval dining halls of London's Inns of Court. Ten stained-glass windows depict Canada's cultural and legal heritage. The wooden railing on the upper floor is carved with ornate crests.

Great Library – Adorned with Corinthian columns, a vaulted ceiling and a large fireplace, this 36.5m by 12m (120ft by 40ft) library is the highlight of Osgoode Hall. Throughout you'll find portraits and busts of chief justices and officers of the Law Society. The library contains one of the biggest collections of legal documents in Canada.

Toronto Reference Library ★

789 Yonge St. 416-395-5577. www.torontopubliclibrary.ca. Open July–Sept Mon–Thu 9:30am–8:30pm, Fri til 5pm, Sat 9am-5pm. Oct-June, Mon–Thu 9:30am–8:30pm, Fri til 5pm. Sun 1:30pm-5pm. Closed holidays.

Need a book? This is the place for you. Canada's largest and most extensive public reference library contains about 1.5 million volumes—not to mention the fact that it's a bustling, popular hang-out.

The large five-storey brick and glass structure (1977) was designed by Raymond Moriyama. Once you're inside, look up to see the tiered balconies that border the wide, light-filled centre.

On the main floor, the Canada Trust Gallery regularly displays materials, often rare, from the library system's myriad collections. In the Map Room on level 4, you'll find antique maps, like those of 17C Canada, as well as charts of the oceans. There's a collection of Science Fiction, Speculation & Fantasy, and another that counts more than 45,000 printed musical scores. A collection of early children's books includes the first Canadian picture book (1859) and even some from the year 1750. In the Canadiana collection you'll discover the country's history and culture, with special focus on genealogy, Ontario history and local history (North York).

It's Elementary, My Dear Watson

To many visitors, the best place in the library lies in a corner on the fifth floor. You'll find a tiny room *(access from 4th floor; open Tue, Thu, Sat 2pm–4pm & by appointment)* filled with the **Arthur Conan Doyle Collection**, the only such collection in the world. Though Doyle wrote about issues of his day, such as crime and spiritualism, he is most famous for his Sherlock Holmes detective stories. The library's collection includes Doyle's autobiography, historical novels, poetry and other writings as well as the books starring Sherlock Holmes. Here in this cozy room you'll see things associated with Holmes, like a smoking pipe, slippers and the inevitable deerstalker on the hat rack. Have a seat on the worn Victorian furnishings and you'll swear the great detective could walk in any minute.

First Floor – Here you'll find the **Directions Desk**, where you can ask staff questions. A number of Canadian and international newspapers, among other periodicals, are available for reading in the **Newspaper Room**. A User Education Centre holds computers that enable visitors to access the library's electronic information system.

Second Floor – The **Main Reference Centre** houses collections in history, science, literature, consumer law and other broad categories. There's a **Travel Area** filled with guides and brochures, and a **Quick Reference Section** stocked with dictionaries, directories and encyclopedias. The **Annex** holds special collections, including books on military topics, fashion, repair manuals and CD-ROMs.

Third Floor – This level contains the **Business Information Centre**, with a **Business Annex** focusing on Canadian companies. A number of computer books are available, as is information on careers and higher education.

Fourth Floor – The **Periodicals Centre** here contains the library's 3,500 magazines, newsletters and journals. Also on this level, the **Special Collections, Genealogy & Map Centre** permits users to access contemporary and historical atlases and maps.

Fifth Floor – This level is occupied by the **Language Learning Centre** and the **Performing Arts Centre,** where you can listen to tapes and CDs. The intriguing **Arthur Conan Doyle Room** *(see sidebar p 34)* fills a cozy corner.

Library Trivia
- 82km/51mi of shelves
- 1,747,331 volumes and bound periodicals
- 2,956,675 other documents (maps, posters, slides, photos, etc.)
- 3,011,569 photocopies
- 1,315,743 questions answered
- 1, 185,286 visitors

Union Station★

65 Front St. W. 416-366-7788. www.ttrly.com. Call for tour information. $5 2-hour guided tours available 11am last Sat. in the month. Reservations required.

This giant of a railway depot extends 229m/751ft—a full city block between Bay and York streets. Opened in 1927, it replaced the outgrown Second Union Station (1872–1931) that occupied Front Street one block to the west. Today it ranks as the largest metropolitan railway station in the country, rising to a height of 34m/112ft at its center. Now a National Historic Site, the station serves as the main passenger depot for intercity and commuter trains. In 2000 the City of Toronto purchased the station, with plans to restore it.

Walk inside the Great Hall, complete with a vaulted ceiling and marble floor from Tennessee.

Facade – The Front Street facade using Indiana and Queenston limestone, is faced with 22 stone columns made from Bedford limestone.

Great Hall – This cavernous hall measures 76m/250ft in length and 25.6m/84ft in width. The coffered, vaulted ceiling rises 26.8m/88ft and is finished with Gustavino tile. At each end of the hall, four-storey-high arched windows flood the interior with light. The walls are constructed of Zumbro stone from Missouri. At street level, the hall functions as a waiting room and ticket-purchase area. Stairs at both ends descend to the Arrivals Concourse. At this level, you can access the subway, Toronto's Underground City and the Royal York Hotel.

A Union Built To Last

His Royal Highness, Edward, the Prince of Wales, remarked at the opening ceremony, August 6, 1927 that the Canadians, "build [their] stations like we build our cathedrals." The long process of building Union Station was sparked by the Great Fire of 1904, which leveled 6ha/14 acres of downtown Toronto. The Canadian Pacific and Grand Trunk Railways took the opportunity to unite and create a new, "union" station. (For decades, each competing railroad line had their own terminal in major cities.) Construction commenced in 1914, and though delayed by wartime shortages, the station was completed in 1921. For another six years, the grand edifice remained empty, before legal conflicts over track alignment were settled. Unique among large-city North American train stations, Union Station relies on efficient through-train operation, not the common stub-end tracks.

Fairmont Royal York Hotel★

100 Front St. W. 416-368-2511. www.fairmont.com/royalyork.

Across the street from Union Station, the Royal York Hotel still courts the travelling public *(see Must Stay)*. It's no coincidence that this landmark sits so close to Union Station: it was built by Canadian Pacific Railway, which constructed the grand hostelries in the Canadian Rockies in the late 1800s.

When the copper-topped building opened its doors in 1929, the Royal York became the tallest skyscraper in the British Commonwealth Empire. Since then, the historic site has hosted countless guests, including Britain's Royal Family, in grand style.

The luxury hotel at the time of its debut boasted such fine amenities as radios in every guest's quarters, and bathrooms with tubs and showers. In addition to 1,000-plus guest rooms, the hotel had a well-stocked library (12,000 volumes), a roof garden, a concert hall and even a small hospital.

When you enter today, you'll be surrounded by crystal chandeliers, plush furniture, and sumptuous wood panelling. Rising 28 stories, the Royal York, now a Fairmont property, is almost a city within itself. On the lower levels, you can browse the shops, dine in one of the many restaurants or enjoy a spa treatment at Elizabeth Milan's Hotel Day Spa *(see Must Be Pampered)*.

What's Royal About The Royal York?

Royalty, Fairmont style, comes in large portions. For example the hotels has:

- 1,365 rooms

- Claims the largest hotel kitchen in Canada, covering over three floors and equal in size to the inside of seven Boeing 747 airplanes

- 6,968sq m/75,000sq ft in 34 banquet and conference rooms

- Serves up to 6,000 meals a day

- Can serve as many as 10,000 people at one meal by using all the public and private dining rooms in the hotel

- Has 72km/45mi of carpeting (about the distance from Toronto to Hamilton)

- 496,000 bottles are collected a year by the hotel staff for recycling

Shoes, sugar, hockey sticks, textiles? What is remarkable about Toronto's museums is their diversity: from Canada's largest repository, the Royal Ontario Museum, with its vast artistic, archaeological and scientific collections, to smaller museums devoted exclusively to shoes and even sugar. These institutions are indeed a boon to tourism, but perhaps the bane of countless school children. Woe to you, if a string of yellow school buses arrives outside the Royal Ontario Museum before you do!

Royal Ontario Museum★★★

100 Queen's Park at Avenue Rd. & Bloor St.W. 416-586-8000. www.rom.on.ca
Open year-round Sat-Thurs 10am–5:30pm (Fri 10am-9:30pm). Closed Jan 1 & Dec 25.
$20 (free 45 min. before closing).

After an ambitious $270-million expansion dubbed Renaissance ROM, in which uber-chic architect Daniel Libeskind designed a crystal façade for the fifth-largest museum in North America, the ROM (pronounced like mom) is ready to awe visitors again. Not since the early 80s when the ROM underwent a major expansion has Toronto encountered such a stir with its beloved institution. With the final galleries scheduled for opening in 2009, the expansion will permit all major collections on permanent display for the first time ever. The new ROM has eight additional galleries, new restaurants, a gift shop and a new entrance, part of the extraordinary Michael Lee-Chin Crystal. The museum, which first opened in 1914 as part of the University of Toronto, displayed treasures from a dynamic young archaeologist from Ontario named Charles Trick Currelly. In the early 1900s he travelled to then-exotic places like Egypt, Crete and Asia Minor. At Abydos in Upper Egypt, he aided in excavation work, amassing rare and wonderful artifacts. Many of the treasures he returned to Canada form the backbone of the ROM's Egyptian gallery. Dr. Currelly also gathered pieces from China, Greece, Italy and other parts of Europe. By 1968, the museum became a separate body under the provincial government.

Galleries are arranged according to the museum's curatorial departments—Biodiversity, Earth Science, Near Eastern and Asian Civilizations, Canadian Heritage and others.

China Trade
The ROM is known especially for its **East Asian collections**, which attract visitors and scholars worldwide. The initial holdings were acquired by luck and quick thinking. Dr. Currelly made a chance acquaintance with a fur dealer/collector named George Crofts, who was living in China. As a result, Crofts shipped a number of works from China in the mid-1920s for the museum's collections. The Anglican Bishop of Hunan Province, William White, returned to Canada and continued to collect works for the ROM after Crofts' death. In 1960 the ROM acquired the collection of Dr. James Menzies, a missionary and scholar who also had resided in China for many years. You can see the fruit of these collective efforts on Level 1 in the East Asia galleries.

Dynamic Earth

Just how amazing is our planet? You'll find out at this exhibit, where you can touch and examine fossils and rocks. And if you like sparkly things, step inside the Mineral Hall to see samples of copper, pyrite, feldspar, galena, quartz and other minerals. You'll ooh and aah at the exquisite gold, diamond, turquoise, jade and other jewellery and gemstones in the S.R. Perren Gem and Gold Room.

Level One – In addition to a new digital gallery allowing visitors to interact with the ROM's collections in virtual 3D, this floor has eight galleries to keep you busy. Be sure to drop by: The **Bishop White Gallery of Chinese Temple Art** boasting three of the world's best-preserved temple wall paintings from the Yuan Dynasty. **The Daphne Cockwell Gallery of Canada: First Peoples** explores aboriginal cultures from 19C to modern day. The **Sigmund Samuel Gallery of Canada** showcases the country's best collection of early Canadiana; while the **Joey and Toby Tanen-**

baum Gallery of China contains 2,500 objects spanning 7,000 years of Chinese history. At the **Prince Takamado Gallery of Japan**, Japanese ceramics, prints and rare artifacts are on display. The **ROM Gallery of Chinese Architecture** possesses the largest collection of Chinese architectural artifacts outside of China and more.

Level Two – Kids will have fun exploring the **CIBC Discovery Gallery** as well as the **Patrick and Barbara Keenan Family Gallery of Hands-on Biodiversity.** They can walk through the Philosophers' Walk Wing, try on field gear and test their flora and fauna skills. Be sure to visit the five other galleries focusing on natural history. The eerie Bat Cave shelters hundreds of handmade bats that appear very lifelike. For dinosaur fans explore the new **James and Louise Temerty Galleries of the Age of Dinosaurs** housing the ROM's renowned dinosaur collection and the new **Gallery of the Age of Mammals** that explores the rise and fall of these now extinct animals.

Level Three - Eight galleries among them are the new **Michael Lee-Chin Crystal Galleries** which will have you browsing for hours. Be sure to visit: the **A.G. Leventis Foundation Gallery of Ancient Cyprus** displaying 300 Cypriot artifacts; **Galleries of Africa, Egypt** showcasing 5,000 years of Egyptian history; **Gallery of the Bronze Age Aegean** examining ancient civilizations of the Cycladic, Minoan, Mycenaean and Geometric periods of Greece; and the **Samuel European Galleries** highlighting European decorative arts from the Middle Ages to modern times.

Level Four – Among the angular walls, corridors and crystal-shaped interior is where the **Institute for Contemporary Culture, the Roloff Beny Gallery** resides, which showcases temporary exhibitions from the world's leading contemporary artists. Later, drop by the **Patricia Harris Gallery of Textiles** and Costume for a glimpse of this fascinating international collection of costume and textiles.

Level Five – At the top floor of Lee-Chin's sits the museum's new restaurant, **C5 ($$$$)**. The setting is stark moderne and is offset by an innovative a la carte menu showcasing local haute cuisine.

Art Gallery of Ontario★★

317 Dundas St. W. 416-979-6648. www.ago.net. Tues-Fri 11am-6pm (Wed until 8:30pm), weekends 10am-5:30pm. $12. Re-opening in mid-2008.

The Art Gallery of Ontario, or the *Eh-Gee-Oh* as locals affectionately call their art gallery, is encountering a six-year make-over dubbed Transformation AGO, which is scheduled for a grand re-opening in mid-2008. Renowned architect Frank Gehry, a former local boy whose family lived down the street from this iconic landmark has undertaken a design to reface and add new galleries to the over 100-year-old historic building, which over the years has encountered previous renovations. Once completed, the AGO will showcase 5,000 artworks in 110 galleries. Other highlights include new public spaces, a dramatic entrance, two restaurants, a shop, film theatre, education centre and a state-of-the-art special events facility. This expansion was sparked by Canadian businessman Kenneth Thomson's donation of 2,000 pieces of art to the AGO in 2003 along with $70-million in funding. The Thomson Collection purported as the most significant private art collection in Canada includes works by Cornelius Krieghoff and members of the Group of Seven, European art objects from medieval times to the mid-19C and a Rubens masterpiece, *The Massacre of the Innocents*.

Besides the Gehry-designed sci-fi facade, visitors will easily recognize the art gallery by the large abstract sculpture at the corner of Dundas and McCaul streets. It's a hint that more works by renowned British sculptor Henry Moore (1898-1986) are inside. The AGO possesses the largest public collection of Moore's works in the world—more than 1,000 items—including 689 prints, 139 original

Mr. Moore's Gift

How did the Henry Moore Collection land in Toronto? After visiting the city to see his sculpture, *The Archer*, installed at the new City Hall, Henry Moore announced in 1968 his gift to the AGO of more than 150 of his works. He had learned that the AGO intended to devote a gallery to him. In 1974 he returned to officially open the new sculpture centre, named in his honor. The artist himself designed the space to use natural light from the glass-panelled roof. The sculptor's gift became a catalyst for the AGO's acquisition of others Modernist sculptures and paintings—including those of Brancusi, Giacometti, Gauguin and Picasso.

plasters and bronzes and 74 drawings. The Gallery's permanent collections total some 26,500 pieces that range from 15C European paintings to international contemporary art. A special focus is Canadian art from the 18C to the present. You can also tour the Grange, the 19C mansion that was the AGO's original home.

Bata Shoe Museum★★

327 Bloor St. 416-979-7799. www.batashoemuseum.ca. Open year-round Mon–Sat 10am–5pm (Thu until 8pm), Sun noon–5pm. Closed major holidays. $12.

Want to see some really unique shoes? Step into this five-storey "shoebox" designed by Raymond Moriyama. The roof's angle and extension create the impression of a lid on a partially opened box. Inside, this museum draws on its

10,000-piece collection to illustrate shoemaking and footwear over a 4,500-year period. Walk up to a pair of 3,550-year-old Theban funerary slippers and 1,500-year-old Anasazi sandals. Stand toe-to-toe with Mahatma Gandhi's leather chappals (c.1940s), Elton John's plat-form shoes, Princess Diana's fuchsia kid pumps, and Pierre Trudeau's leather sandals from his student days. You'll find yourself pointing at bell-adorned padukas worn by brides in India; reed-bound Japanese foot

"buckets" worn to make paths in snow; elevated Italian chopines from Renaissance times; and 19C French clogs with iron spikes for chestnut crushing.

According to Sonja Bata, the founder of the Shoe Museum, "Shoes are such a personal artifact. They tell you about the owner's social status, habits, culture and religion. That's what makes them special." Her marriage to the son of a Czech shoe manufacturer, a Canadian émigré, in 1946 sparked her interest in global footwear. Recognizing that many traditional types were being lost in the name of progress, she travelled the world to find common and extraordinary examples of foot coverings.

Foot Notes

- England's Edward II is given the credit for initiating the measurement of the "foot" in 1320. His own foot measured 36 barley corns; each corn was a third of an inch, making the total of 12 inches equal to one foot.
- In England in the 14C, the length of a shoe's pointed toe was regulated by law and depended upon the wearer's social status.
- The height of a shoe's heel also conveyed the social importance of the wearer. Thus, the wealthy were, and still are, termed "well-heeled."
- The origin of calling someone a "square" is said to derive from the wearing of square-toed shoes long after they were in fashion.

Source: Bata Shoe Museum

Gardiner Museum of Ceramic Art ★★

111 Queen's Park at Avenue Rd. 416-586-8080. www.gardinermuseum.on.ca. Open year–round Mon–Thurs 10am–6pm (Fri until 9pm), weekends 10am–5pm. Closed Jan 1, Nov 12 & Dec 25. $12. Free admission Fridays 4pm-9pm.

A two-year renovation project completed in 2006 has given North America's only specialty ceramics museum a whimsical façade akin to stacked ceramic boxes. The expansion of 14,000 sq.ft/1.3 sq.m provides a dynamic entrance, new galleries, studio spaces, a new retail shop and a funky restaurant helmed by acclaimed chef Jamie Kennedy. The collection houses four major periods including the Ancient Americas, the Italian Renaissance, 17C English pottery, and 18C European porcelain. Toronto philanthropist George R. Gardiner and his wife, Helen, first became interested in ceramics "as a form of decoration." That interest led to collecting and eventually to, as Mr. Gardiner put it, "the opportunity to do something culturally for our country." Their museum, which opened in 1984, features pottery and porcelain from many countries and many cultures. You'll be amazed at the variety: pre-Columbian works dating from 2000 BC, 15C Chinese porcelain, 16C Italian figurines, 17C English earthenware, 18C French porcelains and 18C German decorative works.

Ancient Americas

The Ancient Americas collection houses 340 stunning pieces from Mexico, and Central and South America dating from 2000 BC through the early 1500s. Figurines, vessels and bowls from the Olmec, Toltec and Aztec cultures are highlighted—note the orange Mayan pottery and plumbate (fired with silica glaze) vases.

Asia

Ancient China dominates this stellar collection of porcelain china and other outstanding ceramics dating from as early as the great Ming and Qing Dynasties. Look for the Bell collection of blue and white Chinese porcelain containing nearly 200 pieces including teapots, covered boxes, vases, platters, wine cups and a large pilgrim flask from the Qing Dynasty. Japanese porcelain also receives fine representation with over 30 pieces that include blue-and-white Imari and Kakiemon, a brilliant white porcelain styled with red, turquoise and yellow enamels.

Europe

European ceramics form the majority of the Gardiner Museum's collection. The periods include Italian Renaissance ceramics, 17C and 18C English pottery, and 18C European porcelain mainly from Germany, Austria, France, and England. View 18C porcelains of Du Paquier, Sèvres (identifiable by bright yellow colours), the great English companies—Worcester, Derby, Chelsea—and others. Highlights are the Meissenware pieces, in particular the large tea service (c.1745) in a fitted leather travel case, and the commedia dell'arte figures crafted throughout Europe after this 16C form of improvised theatre spread from Italy. Look for the assembly of tiny, exquisite scent bottles (1715–1765) made largely in England and Germany. The Bell collection of blue-and-white Chinese porcelain contains close to 200 pieces, including teapots, covered boxes, vases, platters, wine cups and a large pilgrim flask from the Qing dynasty.

Contemporary

With a nod to modernism, this ceramic collection of approximately 200 pieces highlights artists from Canada and the United States, as well as internationals. You'll find functional ceramics such as vases, teapots and bowls; sculptural such as abstract; and conceptual pieces.

McMichael Canadian Art Collection★★

Major Mackenzie Dr., Kleinburg. Take Hwy. 400 to Major Mackenzie Dr.; continue west about 6km/4mi to Islington Ave., then go north 1km/.6mi. 905-893-1121. www.mcmichael.com. Open daily 10am–4pm. Closed Dec 25. $15.

It's worth the 40km/25mi drive north to Kleinburg to see this collection. The McMichael showcases one of the world's largest exhibits of paintings by Canada's famed Group of Seven *(see sidebar)*. The wooded hills of the Humber Valley are the setting for the log and fieldstone buildings that hold paintings by the first truly Canadian school. The gallery also owns a sizable collection of contemporary First Nations and Inuit art.

In 1952 Robert and Signe McMichael bought land in rural Kleinburg, decorating their home with Group of Seven paintings. In 1965 they donated their famed collection and property to the province of Ontario. Subsequent gifts by such individuals as automotive industrialist and philanthropist Robert S. McLaughlin have enlarged the collection.

Ground Level – This level is devoted largely to the Group of Seven's precursor, Tom Thomson; to A.Y. Jackson, the "grand old man of Canadian art"; and to

The Group of Seven

Eight Canadian painters are credited with forging a uniquely Canadian art form by painting, in a revolutionary way, the colors and landscapes of the country's wilderness. Though pioneer and avid outdoorsman Tom Thomson (1877–1917) died a mysterious death in the wilderness before the group was formed, his influence was substantial. The original members were Lawren Harris, A.Y. Jackson, J.E.H. MacDonald, Franklin Carmichael, Arthur Lismer, Frederick Varley and Frank Johnston. Johnston left after the first exhibition; A.J. Casson joined the group in 1926. The group officially disbanded in 1932, but some members formed the Canadian Group of Painters, which had much the same aims.

Lawren Harris, the "soul" of the group and a prime leader in Canadian art for decades. Examples by artists influenced by the seven, notably Clarence Gagnon, Emily Carr and David Milne, are also on display.

Upper Level – Here you'll find fine works by contemporary Native artists such as Clifford Maracle, Norval Morrisseau, Daphne Odjig and Arthur Shilling. There are excellent samples of Inuit art as well, principally stone carvings and lithographs.

Hockey Hall of Fame★

[B] *refers to map on inside front cover. Brookfield Place (formerly BCE Place) (lower level), Yonge St. at Front St. 416-360-7765. www.hhof.com. Open late June–Labour Day Mon–Sat 9:30am–6pm, Sun 10am–6pm. Rest of the year Mon–Fri 10am–5pm, Sat 9:30am–6pm, Sun 10:30am–5pm. Closed Jan 1. $13.*

Ever wanted to see the original Stanley Cup? It's on display here in the Hockey Hall of Fame (HHOF), a mecca for hockey fans. Equipment, uniforms, videos of the game's great moments, and even a reproduction of the dressing room for hockey's giants are all here. You can also try out your own hockey skills *(see Musts for Fun)*. After 32 years of residence at Exhibition Place, the Hall opened at Brookfield Place in 1993. In celebration of its tenth anniver-

sary, HHOF upgraded several attractions and added exhibit space in 2003 as part of a $7 million revitalization project.

Take the escalator down one level from the atrium to enter this sporting world, which has been preserved and encased within BCE Place.

What's On Display?

(In addition to an anniversary exhibit, two theatres, a retail store and a resource centre).

Legends Past & Present – Learn about the game's origins, its introduction to North America, and the past season's highlights.

Grand Old Houses of Hockey – Maple Leaf Gardens, Detroit Olympia, Chicago Stadium, Madison Square Garden and other celebrated rinks are lauded here. **Stanley Cup Milestones** includes memorabilia associated with Cup playoffs.

Blockbuster Video Dressing Room – The star of this exhibit is the re-created locker room of the Montreal Canadiens at the Montreal Forum.

Panasonic Hometown Hockey – Displays pay tribute to local and regional clubs and leagues in Canada and the US, as well as equipment.

Royal Canadian Mint World of Hockey – Artifacts and media presentations focus on international hockey, especially World and Olympic Championships.

IBM Global Game Encounter – Interactive exhibit kiosks feature detailed data on international hockey, including honor rolls, tournaments and league play.

WorldCom Great Hall – The domed lobby (1886) of the former Bank of Montreal building holds NHL trophies and the famed Stanley Cup (1892).

The Rest of the Best: Toronto Museums

Museum of Contemporary Canadian Art

952 Queen St.W. 416-395-0067. www.mocca.toronto.on.ca. Open year-round Tues-Sun 11am-6pm; Closed Mon; Free admission.

In 2005 downtown Toronto welcomed this new gallery that once resided in the city's north end. Now a part of Toronto's new trendy district in the hot and hip Art and Design District along Queen Street West, MOCCA celebrates the latest works from Canada's best contemporary artists with works dating from 1985 to today. The permanent collection houses over 400 pieces by more than 140 artists including Edward Burtynsky, Patterson Ewen, and Genevieve Cadieux. Works from leading international artists are also exhibited.

Redpath Sugar Museum

95 Queens Quay E. 416-933-8341. Open year-round Mon–Fri 10am–noon & 1pm–3:30pm.

East of Yonge Street, along Toronto harbour, you can learn all you want to about sugar at the Redpath Refinery's small museum. There are displays on nutrition and the company's founding family as well.

Textile Museum of Canada

55 Centre Ave. 416-599-5321. www.textilemuseum.ca. Open Tue–Fri 11am–5pm (Wed until 8pm), weekends noon–5pm. Closed major holidays. $12; Wed "Pay-what-you-can" admission.

This museum is the only Canadian museum devoted exclusively to the study, collection and display of textiles. It's located on two floors of a high-rise hotel/condominium complex and displays traditional and contemporary works from around the world. The permanent collection of 12,000 pieces is presented on a rotating basis alongside loaned works in temporary exhibits.

Toronto Aerospace Museum

65 Carl Hall Rd., Downsview Airport. 416-638-6078. www.torontoaerospacemuseum.com. Open Thu–Sat 10am–4pm. $8.

Located about 13km/8mi north of the city, this museum celebrates Toronto's aviation and aerospace achievements in the former home of de Havilland Aircraft of Canada, which produced its aircraft here in 1929. Full-size aircraft, engines and original shop equipment are on view.

Toronto takes great pride in its past. While some historic structures have been demolished over the years, public and private efforts have preserved the city's history by restoring many of its architectural treasures. Here are some of the best places to discover Toronto's history.

Black Creek Pioneer Village★★

1000 Murray Ross Pkwy. at Steeles Ave. (29km/18mi northwest of downtown). 416-736-1733. www.blackcreek.ca. Open year-round daily 9:30am–4pm (Jul–Sept until 5pm). Closed Dec 25. $13.

If you want a temporary escape from the fast pace of the city, come to this tranquil 19C village, which opened to the public in 1960. Black Creek re-creates a farming community on 12ha/30 acres, recalling Ontario's rural past. Five of the 40 structures date from the original farm established here by Pennsylvania-German settlers between 1816 and 1832. Other 19C structures were moved to the site.

Stop at the **orientation centre** for a schedule of daily events and activities. Wander the dirt roads flanked by wooden sidewalks and split-rail fences, and feel the charm of a bygone era. Costumed guides are on hand to demonstrate traditional 19C crafts and trade.

Tinsmith Shop – Watch tinsmiths ply their trade.

Stong Farm – Farm buildings and animals form the heart of the village.

Half Way House – This rustic inn, with its two-tiered veranda and stone fireplace, now caters to contemporary diners.

Roblin's Mill – The waterwheel on the four-storey water-powered stone gristmill still turns.

Printing Office – Here you'll see a working flatbed press.

Casa Loma★★

1 Austin Terrace. 416-923-1171.
www.casaloma.org. Open year-round
daily 9:30am–5pm. Closed Jan 1 &
Dec 25. $16.

This enormous 1914 sandstone castle
was home to the prominent industrialist Sir Henry Pellatt. Now it's a
popular tourist attraction. Spanish
for "house on the hill," Casa Loma
stands on the crest of Davenport
Ridge—the edge of glacial Lake
Iroquois, which appeared after the
last Ice Age. Seven storeys high, the
palatial residence has two towers,
which both offer good city views.
Discover the secret passageways and
the underground tunnel that leads to
the magnificent **carriage house**
and stables.

When Money's No Object

Sir Henry Pellatt (1859–1939) amassed a fortune by exploiting Niagara Falls to produce hydroelectricity. As a youth he drew sketches of castles during his world travels. In adulthood, he hired Edward J. Lennox to design a house based on these sketches. Three years, 300 workers and $3.5 million later, the interior was still not finished. Nevertheless, in 1914 Sir Henry and his wife finally moved in. The Pellats' estate was decked out with luxuries that weren't common in pre-World War I homes—an indoor swimming pool, 52 telephones, an elevator, a pipe organ and concealed steam pipes, as well as 21 fireplaces. They stayed in their grand home for less than 10 years, however; the high cost of keeping the house coupled with a reversal in Sir Henry's fortunes led to his losing Casa Loma to the City of Toronto for payment of back taxes.

Casa Loma Highlights

Great Hall – A massive space with a 22m/70ft oak-beamed ceiling, oil portraits, a mounted suit of armour and ornate iron chandeliers.

Conservatory – The centrepiece here is the lovely stained-glass dome; an Italian-marble-floor lies beneath it.

Library – Glass-enclosed shelves with space for 10,000 books line the walls.

Round Room – Shaped to fit within the tower, this space is appointed with exquisite Louis XV furnishings.

Sir Henry's Bedroom – Sir Henry slept in this 18m by 13m (60ft by 40ft) mahogany- and walnut-panelled bed chamber, complete with dressing room, bathroom and a balcony above the Great Hall.

Campbell House★

160 Queen St. 416-597-0227. www.campbellhousemuseum.ca. Visit by guided tour only, mid-May–mid-Oct Tues–Fri 9:30am–4:30pm. Closed Jan 1 & Dec 25–26. $4.50.

The oldest remaining building from the original town of York was built in 1822 for Sir William Campbell (1758–1834), who served as the chief justice of Upper Canada (now Ontario) from 1825 to 1829. When he retired from public service in 1829, Campbell was knighted for his contributions to local politics, law and religion.

The Georgian brick mansion was moved to this site in 1972 from its location on Adelaide Street in historic York. Steps away from the city's courthouse, where Sir William worked. After meticulous restoration, the residence opened to the public in 1974 by the Queen Mother.

Rooms contain some fine period pieces (none of the original furniture remains) and original portraits of the Campbell family.

Previous Owners

The property once belonged to the Canada Life Assurance Company, whose headquarters rise just behind Campbell House. A prominent landmark, the Canada Life building is easily recognizable at night by its lighted tower. The tower's lights indicate the barometer reading.

The Distillery Historic District★

55 Mill St. at Parliament St. 416-364-1177. www.thedistillerydistrict.com. Open year-round Sun–Wed 11am–7pm, Thu–Sat 11am–9pm.

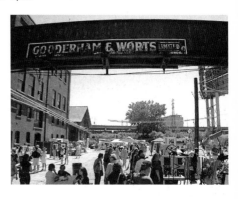

One of Toronto's oldest historical complexes is also the city's newest centre for arts and entertainment. A stop at the visitor centre located in the Stables is a good way to start any visit. Billed as the largest and best-preserved collection of Victorian Industrial architecture in North America, the Distillery sits on 13 acres in the downtown core. The $20 million project consists of 44 historic buildings linked by bricked streets surrounding a large central courtyard. The property dates back to 1837 when brothers-in-law William Gooderham and James Worts got the idea to turn surplus grain from an 1832 mill here into whisky. Gooderham and Worts Distillery soon became the largest in the British Empire. The Distillery also hosts festivals and special events, such as arts festivals, antique and vintage auto shows, outdoor art exhibits, wine tastings and film screenings. The complex has also appeared in a number of recent films, including *Chicago* and *X-Men*.

Where Can I Eat?

The Boiler House – Located in the Boiler House complex, the restaurant offers a succulent contemporary Canadian menu.

Mill Street Brewery – *Paint Shop*. Beer connoisseurs will appreciate this boutique micro brewery.

Pure Spirits Oyster House & Grill – *Pure Spirits building*. Oysters rule the day here.

Brick Street Bakery – *Boiler House complex*. Treat yourself to a flaky pastry or a fresh sandwich.

Balzac's Coffee House – *Pump House*. The classic coffeehouse is named for French writer and coffee-lover Honoré de Balzac.

> **Gallery Picks**
> **Sandra Ainsley Gallery**, housed in the Cooperage, showcases glass art from around the world. **Corkin /Shopland Gallery**, exhibiting the works of vintage and modern photographers, is located in the 1870 Pure Spirits building. The Tank House contains the **Museum of Contemporary Art**.

Elgin and Winter Garden Theatre★

189 Yonge St., opposite Eaton Centre. 416-314-2901. www.heritagefdn.on.ca.
Visit by guided tour only, year-round Thu 5pm & Sat 11am. Closed Dec 25. $10.

Ever heard of a double-decker theatre? This splendid structure houses the last remaining double-decker theatres in the world. The 1,500-seat Elgin and 1,000-seat Winter Garden were both designed by Thomas Lamb. In 1913 and 1914 respectively, they opened as vaudeville theatres and later became silent-film houses. The Winter Garden closed in 1928 and the Elgin became a movie palace. They were brought back to life after an extensive two-year restoration and reopened in 1989. Since then, the centre has been staging new and traditional plays and musicals on a regular basis. Step inside to see the Elgin's gilded lobby with its Corinthian pilasters and arched mirrors; then head into the Elgin's plush amphitheatre, which features ornate box seats and a gold-patterned ceiling. A seven-storey marble staircase leads up to the fanciful Winter Garden, with its unique ceiling of hanging beech boughs and twinkling lights. Don't miss the original hand-painted scenic backdrops that are on display in the lobby and lounge areas.

How Do You Spruce Up A Theatre?

You'll need lots of money, plenty of elbow grease, sheets of aluminum leaf and—bread dough! After purchasing the theatre building in 1981, the Ontario Heritage Foundation began a $30 million renovation (1987–1989) of the two theatres. Some 300,000 razor-thin sheets of aluminum leaf were needed to restore the gilt work in the Elgin. Bread dough—made from 1,500 pounds of flour—was used to clean the Winter Garden's walls and restore their original hand-painted garden scenes. As part of the 6,038sq m/65,000sq ft expansion, a new lobby, lounges, and a backstage—a full eight-storeys high—were added.

Fort York★

100 Garrison Rd. 416-392-6907. www.toronto.ca/culture/fort_york. Open Victoria Day–Labour Day daily 10am–5pm. Rest of the year daily 10am–4pm. Closed mid-Dec–Jan 1. $6.

Dwarfed by the city's towering skyline, this historic garrison on the outskirts of downtown recalls the humble beginnings of Toronto more than 200 years ago. Once strategically positioned on Lake Ontario's edge, Fort York guarded Toronto's harbour and its earliest settlement.

In 1793 British lieutenant governor John Graves Simcoe had the post constructed as a temporary log garrison. To control Lake Ontario during times of war, Simcoe wanted to build a naval base. However, a number of factors, including lack of money, prevented him from constructing permanent defences. In 1811, when British-American relations soured, the deteriorating barracks of Fort York had to be moved eastward and fortified. After a brief American occupation in April 1813, the fort was rebuilt by the British. As US threats subsided, the fort's military importance diminished. For the city's centennial in 1934, Fort York was renovated and opened as a museum.

Costumed staff members conduct tours and demonstrate baking, butter-making and other 18C chores.

If you're visiting Toronto in the summer *(Jul–Aug)*, be sure to catch the military manoeuvres staged at the fort.

Brick Barracks – These two buildings, completed in 1815, each housed up to 35 soldiers and their families.

Officers' Barracks – Constructed in 1815 (expanded in 1829), the officer's barracks is furnished to show the lifestyle of senior officers.

Junior Officers' Barracks – The 1930s barracks incorporates materials from a 19C building.

Blockhouses – Two early fortifications remain; both were constructed in 1813 and have two levels.

Magazines – After 1824 the 1814 brick magazine served as a weapons depot. Bombproof and well-ventilated, the 1815 stone powder magazine kept gunpowder dry.

Under Attack

In April, 1813—during the War of 1812—an American force with 1,750 soldiers landed west of the fort and was backed by 14 ships mounted with 83 cannons. A combined British, Canadian and Native American defensive, involving 400 men and 12 cannons, failed to halt the enemy's advance, despite the subsequent arrival of a 300-man-strong militia. After the British commander ordered a retreat and the demolition of the gunpowder magazine, the militia surrendered. Some 157 defenders and 320 Americans lost their lives. In December 1814, the war finally ended.

Mackenzie House★

*82 Bond St. 416-392-6915. www.toronto.
ca/culture/mackenzie_house.
Open May–Sept Tue–Sun noon–5pm.
Rest of the year weekends noon–5pm.
Closed major holidays. $4.*

If these walls could talk! This house was the last residence of firebrand **William Lyon Mackenzie** (1795–1861).
Two years before Mackenzie's death, his friends purchased the 19C brick row house (1857) for the outspoken Scotsman who was Toronto's first mayor *(see History)*. Originally, the residence consisted of three row houses, but two fell to the wrecking ball in the 1930s. The remaining one, with its four chimneys, is remarkable for the front lawn that separates it from the street, a rare configuration in the mid-19C. Not once, but twice (in 1932 and in the 1950s), public-minded residents saved Mackenzie's house from demolition. Rooms on all three floors have been restored to the 1850s period.

Kitchen – Sample goodies made according to 19C recipes and baked in the cast-iron oven.

Upstairs Parlor – Here Mackenzie and his cronies would discuss the day's political events.

Print Shop – In the replica print shop, you can watch volunteers work the hand-operated flatbed press on which Mackenzie printed his newspaper.

Annex – Displays in the modern annex detail Mackenzie's life and times.

Power to the People

Born in Dundee, Scotland, William Mackenzie emigrated to Canada in 1820. There he established a newspaper, the *Colonial Advocate*, which became the forum for his dim views about the ruling government of York. In 1837 Mackenzie published a declaration of Canadian independence and shortly thereafter led an armed rebellion to take over the city. After an unsuccessful skirmish with British forces, Mackenzie fled to the US. His efforts, however, were not in vain. The British Parliament ultimately granted "responsible government" to the Canadian colonies, and in 1849 Mackenzie was permitted to return to Canada.

Old Town Toronto ★

Bounded by Front, George, Adelaide & Berkeley Sts. www.oldtowntoronto1793.com.

Toronto had its beginnings in this 10-block area bordering Lake Ontario. In 1793 Lieutenant Governor Simcoe approved a surveyor's grid-iron plan for the temporary capital of Upper Canada (now Ontario). The settlement was named York, for the son of King George III. Although not original to Simcoe's town, some remaining historic structures, such as the bustling **South St. Lawrence Market** *(Front St. E. at Jarvis St.),* date from the first half of the 19C. Within the market you can see the surviving portion of the **Second City Hall** (1899); nearby on Wellington Street at Front Street, Toronto's flatiron building, the Gooderham, dates to 1892. Identifiable by its domed cupola, Neoclassical **St. Lawrence Hall** (1850) at King and Jarvis streets is the former site of the city's market.

First Post Office ★ – *260 Adelaide St. E. Open year-round Mon–Fri 9am–4pm, weekends 10am–4pm. Closed major holidays.* The first post office for the newly incorporated city of Toronto (1834) is now re-created to the period and staffed with costumed interpreters. Inside you'll find replicas of the original mail boxes and a reading room where city residents once perused their mail.

Yonge Street – West of Old York stretches one of the longest roads (1,896km/1,178mi) in Canada. The city's east-west dividing line, Yonge Street was built by Simcoe in 1795 as a military route. Now boutiques, flower stands, trendy restaurants and antiques shops abound along its city blocks.

Letters 1830's Style

Ever wonder how people wrote letters hundreds of years before they had PCs? They used quill pens, of course. In the reading room at Toronto's First Post Office, you can write a 19C-style letter, too *($1 fee)*. Write your message with the quill, then pour sand over what you've written and shake it off. Fold the paper and seal it with wax (there were no envelopes in the early 19C). Before you send it, have the letter hand-stamped with the post office's unique "York-Toronto 1833" cancellation.

Spadina House and Museum★

285 Spadina Rd. 416-392-6910. www.toronto.ca/culture/spadina.htm. Visit by guided tour only, May–Labour Day Tue–Sun noon–5pm. Rest of Sept–Dec Tue–Fri noon–4pm, weekends noon–5pm. Closed major holidays. $6.

Not far from Casa Loma stands the former home of businessman James Austin. Built on a 32ha/80-acre hillside estate outside mid-19C Toronto, Spadina now stands on 2.5ha/6 acres in a fashionable residential district. Austin acquired the estate in 1866, and replaced the existing dwelling with a new Georgian-style house. Head of (1874–1897)—the Consumers' Gas Company, he later founded Dominion Bank and served as its first president. Highlights include the spacious drawing room with its matching red-and-white striped seating, and the wicker-furnished palm room.

The Carlu

444 Yonge St., 7th Floor. 416-597-1931. www.thecarlu.com.

Said to be the inspiration for the Rainbow Room in New York City's Rockefeller Center, this long-anticipated special-events venue has now reopened to the public. In its early-20C heyday, the 4,645sq m/50,000sq ft space on the seventh floor of the former Eaton building (c.1930s) held private dining rooms. Its 1,200-seat concert hall hosted the likes of Glenn Gould, Duke Ellington and Billie Holiday before closing its doors in 1979. In collaboration with Lady Eaton, French architect Jacques Carlu designed the interior of the 1929 building in the Art Moderne style.

North Toronto Railway Station

10 Scrivener Square. 416-922-0403. www.lcbo.com.

Newly restored to its former glory, the railway station houses Canada's largest (2,880sq m/31,000sq ft) and most unique liquor store, the **Liquor Control Board of Ontario-LCBO**. Look beyond the bottles to its magnificent cathedral ceiling, marble walls and brass ticket wickets hidden from view for more than 60 years. The store stocks an estimated 5,500 wines, spirits and beers from some 70 countries, and includes a great selection of Ontario wines and late-harvest ice wine. Special features include wine-tasting stations, cooking classes and wine-appreciation courses.

Toronto enjoys over 8,094 hectares/20,000 acres of grassy urban spaces—spreading from Centre Island to the far corners of the city limit.

For details about the city's parks, contact Toronto Parks & Recreation: 416-392-8186; www.city.toronto.on.ca/parks.

Toronto Islands★★

Offshore, south of Queen's Quay E. Island ferries depart from downtown Toronto at the foot of Bay St. (see Neighbourhoods).

Queen's Park★

Queen's Park Crescent between College & Bloor Sts.

Situated in downtown Toronto, this park is home to the massive sandstone Legislative Buildings of Ontario Parliament. Named in honor of Queen Victoria, Queen's Park was originally called University Park. In 1860 Victoria's son, Albert Edward, Prince of Wales, renamed and dedicated the park for "the recreation of the citizens."

Don River Valley

East of downtown, along Broadview Ave., north of Gerrard St. E.

Travel along the banks of the Don River, just east of the downtown core. Part of the City of Toronto's Discovery Walks program *(see sidebar, opposite)*, this valley embraces steep tributary ravines, native tree species, Riverdale Farm *(see Musts for Kids)*, a 1910 viaduct, 18C mills and marshland. The wetland environment provides great bird-watching.

Don Valley Brick Works Park

Located on the west side of Bayview Ave., just south of Pottery Rd. 550 Bayview Ave. 416-596-1495. www.evergreen.ca/rethinkspace.

Toronto's many buildings possess brick exteriors that are synonymous from these bricks that were created at the Don Valley Brick Works Factory, a brick making and quarry site. Situated in a valley by the Don River, the 340,000 sq ft industrial site of 15 buildings was in business from 1889 until 1984. It stood vacant until a group of environmentalists and community activists recently revived the derelict buildings as a park. Billed as "a destination for families and individuals to enjoy a natural refuge," visitors enjoy nature and culture as they explore the park and the special events throughout the year. Highlights include a weekend farmer's market, event spaces for theatre, a public rooftop garden, and environmental programs such as wetlands restoration.

Allan Gardens

Sherbourne & Carlton Sts. Daily 10am-5pm. 416-392-7288. www.toronto.ca/parks/parks_gardens/allangdns.htm.

One of Toronto's early politicians George W. Allan donated this site to the Toronto Horticultural Society which in turn opened this Victorian conservancy called the Palm House in 1910. While the doggy-set and downtrodden have been known to frequent this patch of green in downtown, the park is currently undergoing a heritage garden conservation project in preparation for its upcoming centennial in 2010.

High Park

1873 Bloor St. W. www.highpark.org.

Considered the jewel of Toronto's park system, High Park has attracted picnickers, families, and brides and grooms for years. The growing environmental trend has also spawned a network of naturalists studying the unique flora and fauna of this 164-hectare/400-acre park in the city's west end.

Home to one of North America's most endangered habitats, the oak savannah, the park also houses an extraordinary petting zoo. In summer, theatre-goers watch "Shakespeare in the Park," a popular outdoor theatre program. Bike paths, pedestrian trails and boardwalks pass through forests, popular Grenadier Pond, and Colborne Lodge. Architect John Howard purchased 165-acres stretching from the lake to Bloor Street in 1836 and designed and lived at this Regency-style cottage he named Colborne Lodge with his wife Jemima. Over the years, he purchased additional land and decided to deed some property along with his cottage to the city on the condition that it remain a natural park free to the people.

Humber River Valley

West of downtown, along Riverside Dr.

The east bank of the Humber River (along Riverside Dr.) follows a trade route long travelled by Toronto's early peoples. Among the city's greening goals is the ongoing naturalization of the shores of the Humber River, one of Canada's official heritage rivers. French explorer Etienne Brule was the first European to traverse the Humber and survey the area which later became the future site of Toronto. The winding 10.5km/6.5mi **Humber Valley Trail** draws hikers, cyclists and in-line skaters.

Humber River Walk

For a shorter route than the Humber Valley trail, begin this 7.3km/4.5mi signed **Discovery Walk** at the banks of the Humber, just north of Bloor Street, near the Old Mill Subway Station. Heading south toward Lake Ontario, you'll pass the remains of an old mill, a stone bridge (1916), the marshes near the river's mouth and the site of a mid-18C French trading post. Near the Queensway, veer right (west) and head northwest through South Humber Park. Stay parallel to Stephen Drive and continue north through King's Mill Park to return to the trailhead.

Toronto Music Garden

475 Queen's Quay W. between Bathurst St. and Spadina Ave. Open year round. Free. 416.973.4000 www.toronto.ca/parks/music_index.htm

Taking inspiration from Bach's *First Suite for Unaccompanied Cello*, cellist Yo-Yo Ma and landscape designer Julie Messervy created the Toronto Music Garden. Overlooking the waterfront, the urban park celebrates the composition by using a series of paths. View granite boulders, hackberry trees; Walk through a wildflower meadow and birch forest. During summer, free music and dance programming along with guided and self-guided tours by Harbourfront Centre are offered.

Rouge Park

Kingston Rd. (Hwy. 2), east of Sheppard Ave. (Port Union Exit off Hwy. 401). 905-713-6038. www.rougepark.com.

Looking to set up camp, but not too far from Toronto? Located east of downtown, the 4,800-hectare/11,856-acre Rouge Park is North America's largest natural-environment park in an urban area. It is also the city's only park with campsites, hot showers and toilets. Highlights include bird-watching, hiking trails, picnic areas, and great views of Lake Ontario and the river.

Scarborough's Parks

About 14km/9mi east of downtown Toronto. 416-338-0338. www.city.toronto.on.ca.

East of Toronto lies sprawling Scarborough, an urban centre known for its picturesque cliffs along Lake Ontario. Toronto's most dramatic geographical feature, the **Scarborough Bluffs** protrude into the lake for about 16km/10mi along its shoreline.

- **Scarborough Bluffs Park** *(from Kingston Rd., turn left on Midland Ave., then immediate left onto Kelsonia and right onto Scarborough Crescent)* offers fine **views**★ of the high sand structures branching out from the cliffs.

- **Bluffers Park** *(from Kingston Rd., travel east to Brimley Rd. and turn right; 416-392-8186)*, with its striking topography, is the most visually unique park in Toronto. Dating to the last Ice Age, the park's landmark bluffs rise sharply about 8km/13mi above the beach.

- **Spencer Clark Collection of Historic Architecture**★ *(Guild Inn, 201 Guildwood Pkwy. off Kingston Rd.; 416-261-3331)* is a sculpture park. Located on the grounds of the Guild Inn, the park displays architectural elements rescued from over 50 demolished Toronto buildings by Rosa and Spencer Clark.

Tommy Thompson Park

Leslie St. & Lakeshore Blvd. 416-667-6299. www.trca.on.ca. Open weekends only.

Built on a 5km/8mi-long man-made peninsula jutting out into Lake Ontario, Tommy Thompson Park is a designated Important Bird Area (IBA) and home to a large population of inland seagulls. The park's meadows, forests and wetlands have attracted nearly 300 species of birds.

As a vibrant, multicultural city with a stimulating mix of indigenous and imported cultures, Toronto boasts several distinct neighbourhoods. Some of them centre on shopping, like Kensington Market and Yorkville. Others, such as Chinatown, Little Italy and the Greek district, draw on the ethnic background of their inhabitants. The formerly Irish enclave of Cabbagetown and the Toronto Islands' small but close-knit community share a sense of place.

Getting There

Ferries to the Toronto Islands depart from the ferry docks at the foot of Bay Street on Queen's Quay. The boats run to three different points: Centre Island, Ward's Island and Hanlan's Point. Ferries run year-round daily 6:35am–11:45pm; $6 round-trip. *For more information and detailed schedules, call 416-392-8193 or check online at www.toronto.ca.*

Toronto Islands★★

Offshore, south of Queen's Quay East. Island ferries depart from the foot of Bay St.

Looking for recreation in Toronto? The three main Toronto islands—Centre, Ward's and Algonquin—function as the city's principal public parkland, but they also shelter a community of year-round cottage dwellers and house boaters.

These narrow landmasses located just offshore from downtown formed a peninsula until 1853, when a violent storm severed it from the mainland, creating the present string of islands. Extending 6km/3.7mi from end to end, the islands are graced with expansive lawns, age-old shade trees, sandy beaches, marinas and splendid views of downtown. Algonquin and Ward's islands, rimmed with quaint roads lined with small cottages, have a rural charm. Attractions on Centre Island include restaurants, cafes, a beach (on the Lake Ontario side) and a delightful amusement park for youngsters *(see Musts for Kids)*. Motor vehicles are prohibited on the islands. A small

airport is located on the western end at Hanlan's Point, known for its fine views of the city. Between Hanlan's Point and Centre Island a trackless train operates continuously.

In the early 1900s, well-to-do Torontonians summered on the islands, while others headed there for weekend getaways. When government plans called for the removal of dwellings to completely convert the islands to parkland, many island home owners refused to leave. Now residents lease the land from the local government. As you stroll or pedal the pathways by rented bicycle, you'll recognize pride of ownership in the well-tended grounds and flower gardens of these woodsy cottages. Only a short ferry ride away from the mainland, the Toronto Islands remain a popular retreat from the frantic pace of the city.

Yorkville★

Yorkville Ave. between Yonge St. & Avenue Rd.

Once the hangout of drug addicts and dropouts, Yorkville has undergone a remarkable transformation and today it represents all that is chic in Toronto. Between Yonge Street and Avenue Road, Yorkville Avenue is lined with charming Victorian houses that have been converted to expensive boutiques, trendy cafes and cutting-edge hair salons. In York Square at the corner of Avenue Road and Yorkville Avenue, shops surround an interior brick courtyard where summer dining is alfresco. Behind the square lies posh **Hazelton Lanes** *(see Must Shop)*, a labyrinthian shopping/office/condominium complex (1978) designed by Boris Zerafa. On the other side of Yorkville Avenue, Cumberland Court is a rambling enclosure of old and new shops, eateries and offices, with a passageway to Cumberland Street. If you wander the quiet, tree-lined residential streets just north of Yorkville Avenue, you'll find upscale urban dwellings fronted by well-manicured grounds.

Cabbagetown

East of Parliament St., between Wellesley & Dundas St. East.

This former working-class enclave has been transformed into a neighbourhood of green spaces, tree-lined streets and renovated Victorian homes, many dating to the 1890s. It's believed that the town's name originated from the cabbages that sprouted in the front yards of immigrant families. The main thoroughfare, Parliament Street, once held the original government buildings (1794–1797) of Upper Canada. Today a diverse population calls Cabbagetown home. Restaurants here include Ethiopian, Japanese, Chinese, French, Italian and more. In addition to colourful shops and restaurants, places of note include the turn-of-the-19C Riverdale Farm, site of the original Toronto Zoo, and Allan Gardens *(see Parks and Gardens)*. Among those laid to rest in Cabbagetown's Necropolis Cemetery *(Winchester & Sumach Sts.)* is Toronto's first mayor, William Lyon Mackenzie *(see History)*.

Chinatown

Dundas St. from Elizabeth St. to Spadina Ave.

Chinatown is the centre of the city's growing Chinese community—and one of the largest Chinese districts in North America. This bustling quarter is alive with street vendors, most notably produce merchants, whose fresh fruits and vegetables fill wooden bins outside their shops. Many restaurants and stores sell Asian foods and wares, attracting a growing number of visitors as well as local residents. The neighbourhood is a wonderful place for a daytime stroll year-round. Browse the food stalls, gift shops and flower stands to experience the aromas and sounds of this boisterous district. Particularly lively during **Chinese New Year** *(see Calendar of Events)*, Chinatown is the site of the **Dragon Dance Parade**, when colourful, handmade dragons wind through the streets to the beat of drums to assure the community's prosperity in the coming year.

Greektown

Danforth Ave. between Chester St. & Broadview Ave. www.greektowntoronto.com.

Another of Toronto's enjoyable walking neighbourhoods, the **Danforth Avenue** section known as **Greektown** is lined with designer shops, stylish restaurants (many offering sidewalk patios and open kitchens), pastry shops, numerous cafes and fruit markets overflowing with Greek food products. The national flag of Greece is omnipresent and streets are signed in Greek as well as in English. Popular eateries include **Myth** *(417 Danforth Ave., see Must Eat)*, and **Pappas Grill** *(440 Danforth; see Must Eat)*, best known for appetizers like homemade hummus and tzatziki dips and clay-oven-baked pizzas.

The specialty shop **Romancing the Home** *(511 Danforth Ave.)* stocks unique gifts and designer household items. Travelling with the kids? They'll love **Suckers** *(450 Danforth Ave.)*, a sweet shop brimming with candy, toys and premium ice cream. For great family fun, catch the annual **Taste of the Danforth** *(see Calendar of Events)*, which turns this busy thoroughfare into a pedestrian walkway bursting with live entertainment, food stalls from most of the restaurants, music, and fashion shows.

Kensington Market

Kensington Ave., west of Spadina Ave. and north of Dundas St.

Primarily a Jewish marketplace in the 1920s, Kensington Market is now largely the realm of the Portuguese, East Indian and Caribbean communities. A jumble of several adjacent streets bustling with outdoor and indoor vendors, the market attracts crowds of bargain-seeking shoppers and tourists. The push-carts of the early 20C have been replaced by fresh fruit and vegetable stands, bakeries, cheese shops, imported food boutiques and small grocery stores that line the streets. Second-hand and vintage clothing outlets like Courage My Love *(14 Kensington Ave.)*, Vintage Depot *(70 Kensington Ave.)* and Planet Aid *(160 Baldwin St.)* draw repeat patrons. Monday through Saturday mornings is the best time to visit the market. On December 21, after sundown, Kensington Market is the setting for the **Kensington Karnival**, which celebrates the winter solstice, complete with a mummers' parade.

Little India

Gerrard St. between Woodfield & Coxwell. www.gerrardindianbazaar.com.

Gerrard Indian Bazaar, or Little India as it's also called, is an East Toronto neighbourhood filled with East Indians, Pakistanis and Bengali families, plus a good mix of other nationalities. The stretch of Gerrard Street between Woodfield and Coxwell is where you'll find a concentration of about 100 Indian, Pakistani, Sri Lankan and Bangladeshi stores. Food markets, dessert and pastry shops and fabric stores, among others, display their wares here. Jewellery shops flash rows of gold baubles, bridal boutiques flaunt dresses for an entire wedding party, while many stores sell brightly coloured silk saris and other traditional fashions and accessories. Over 50 Indian restaurants occupy this strip, including the locally popular Gerrard Street East trio **New Haandi** *(no. 1401),* **Bombay Bhel** *(no. 1411)* and **Motimahal** *(no. 1422).* You'll find bargain buffets in Little India, too. Some of the restaurants are open late and offer live performances of classical Indian music. Stock up on spices and condiments at **Kohinoor Foods** or sample sweet grilled corn-on-the-cob sold at sidewalk barbecues. In May the neighbourhood celebrates **South Asian Heritage Month** with a popular street festival.

Little Italy

College St. from Euclid Ave. to Shaw St.

Little Italy, and farther north, **Corso Italia** *(see sidebar)*, have traditionally been the city's two Italian districts. In recent times, Little Italy has seen an influx of Portuguese and Asian residents who have brought their native cuisine to join the area's Italian restaurants. Coffeehouses and bistros mix in with home-decor shops, art galleries, grocery stores and bakeries. The area has also become one of Toronto's hottest night spots: **College Street** *(from Bathurst to Shaw Sts.)* hosts a variety of new restaurants and trendy bars *(see Nightlife)* that attract evening and weekend revelers, especially college students and the martini crowd, to places like Butt'r, Veni Vidi Vici and Diplomatico's. The area is so dense with restaurants and bistros that real-estate agents are beginning to refer to the strip as Restaurant Row.

Corso Italia

St. Clair Ave., west of Bathurst St. to Lansdowne Ave.

This neighborhood has a greater concentration of Italians than even Little Italy. Here family-run restaurants and fashionable cafes spill out onto the sidewalk, and churches are interspersed among fish markets, grocery shops, coffeehouses and bakeries. Take a leisurely walk to appreciate the daily life of the city's Italian community; be sure to stop for a cup of cappuccino and a cannoli, or try an exotic flavour at one of Corso Italia's gelaterias.

Despite its sophistication, Toronto is one big toy box of kid-loving attractions that will keep children occupied for hours. The only requirements are friendly adult supervision (at least for the younger ones), transportation, money for the admission fee, and a little bit of patience. Here are some sure-fire pleasers.

Toronto Zoo★★★

Meadowvale Rd., Scarborough. 416-392-5900. www.torontozoo.com. Open year-round daily 9am (Oct–Mar 9:30am); closing times vary. Closed Dec 25. $20 adults, $12 children (ages 4-12).

Divided into six "zoogeographic" regions (Africa, Australasia, Eurasia, the Americas, Indo-Malaya and Canada), this world-class zoo covers 287ha/710 acres. Hop on the **Zoomobile** *($7)* to get the big picture first. Step off at the Serengeti station and start walking. You may not see all 5,000 animals, but you'll see many of them, even some endangered or rare animals like two Siberian tiger cubs born at the zoo, and the snow leopard.

What's Cool At The Zoo?

• Filled with tropical vegetation and exotic birds, the **Africa Pavilion** is home to lowland gorillas.

• Near the **Gorilla Rainforest**, be on the lookout for Canada's largest herd of African elephants.

• See if you can spot a seldom-seen Tasmanian devil in **The Edge of Night** exhibit at the Australasia Pavilion.

Ontario Science Centre By The Letters
The centre's four levels of exhibits are identified by letters B through E.
Level B – Changing exhibits fill the P&G Great Hall.
Level C – Would-be astronauts can strap themselves into the rocket chair and virtually explore the moon in the **Space** exhibit.
Level D – Make your hair stand on end with the **Van de Graaff Generator** in the Science Arcade.
Level E – Climb a rock wall or try to beat the recorded time of wheelchair athletes in the Sportschair Sprint in the **Sports** area.

Ontario Science Centre★★★

770 Don Mills Rd. 416-696-1000. www.ontariosciencecentre.ca. Open year-round daily 10am–5pm. Closed Dec 25. $17 adults, $12.50 children (ages 13-17), $10 children (ages 5-12). Additional fee for OMNIMAX films.

Cascading down the Don River ravine, this Raymond Moriyama-designed complex provides great family fun. Push buttons, rotate cranks, pedal a bicycle and turn wheels. Activities are hands-on at this science and technology exhibit. With over 600 exhibits, the centre will have you returning for more.

Black Creek Pioneer Village★★

1000 Murray Ross Pkwy. 416-736-1733. www.blackcreek.ca. Open May–June 30 daily 9:30am–4pm; July 1-Sept 9:30am-5pm. Closed Dec 25. $13 adults, $6 children (ages 5-14), $6 parking.

What was it like having to weave your own fabric and raise your own animals? You'll find out as you tour this living pioneer village and chat with costumed farmers. The early settlement site also provides special events throughout the year.

Pioneer Village Highlights

Strong Farm – Visit this original farm established in 1816 by Pennsylvania-German settlers.

Half Way House – This spacious inn boasts a two-level veranda.

Roblin's Mill – Visit this four-storey water-powered stone gristmill.

Printing Office – Watch a flatbed press in action.

Harbourfront Centre★★

235 Queen's Quay W. 416-973-4000. www.harbourfrontcentre.com. Schedule and prices vary, depending on event. Tickets are available at the box office (open Tue–Sun 1pm–8pm) or online.

Culture *can* be fun for kids throughout the summer, during festival season when dance, theatre, and arts and crafts are celebrated. An additional series of festivals (Hot & Spicy Food, South Asian, Blues) provides summer fun for families; admission (for the most part) is free.

Ontario Place★★

955 Lakeshore Blvd. W., access from Exhibition Grounds. 416-314-9900. www.ontarioplace.com. Grounds and most attractions open daily mid-May–Aug (Sept weekends only) at 10am. Closing times vary. $12.75 adults, $6.75 children (4-5) (additional fees apply for individual attractions).

This mega-playground is packed with adventure. Try the water park with wading pools and water jets, pedal and bumper boats, or a water slide. There's even mini-golf, helicopter rides, a children's village, and a 3D Cinesphere Theatre showcasing IMAX films.

Centreville Amusement Park

Centre Island. 416-203-0405. www.centreisland.ca. Open May–Sept daily 10:30am. Closing times vary. $27.50 adults, $19 children (under 4ft tall).

This one's for the 12-and-under set. Chug around the park on the Centreville train, then head over to the amusement park which has over 30 kiddie rides. Go for a spin on the Ferris wheel, board the log water ride, bumper cars or bumper boats. There's also miniature golf, a games arcade and typical amusement-park goodies like candy apples and cotton candy. Nearby, children will love the petting zoo at Far Enough Farm, filled with barnyard animals, and a hedge maze—perfect for getting lost and found. When it's time to eat, choose one of the three restaurants, the Carousel Café, the Island Paradise, and the Beach House Café.

Playdium

99 Rathburn Rd. W. 905-273-9000. www.playdium.com. Open year-round Mon–Thu noon–11pm, Fri noon–1am, Sat 10am–1am, Sun 10am–11pm. Playcards vary from $20 to $30.

More than 200 video games and simulated rides (think virtual roller coaster) will guarantee to glaze over any kid's eyes. If you prefer the real thing, there's a rock-climbing wall, batting cages, go-carts and an 18-hole mini putt.

Riverdale Farm

201 Winchester St. at Sumach Sts. 416-392-6794. www.city.toronto.on.ca/parks/riverdalefarm.htm. Open daily 9am–5pm.

Nestled on the former site of the Toronto Zoo, this urban farm comes complete with farm animals. Milk a cow, collect eggs, and get close to chickens, pigs and goats. Open year-round near downtown, Riverdale Farm offers self-guided tours.

Wild Water Kingdom

7855 Finch Ave., West Brampton. 416-369-0123. 866-900-9453. www.wildwaterkingdom.com. Open daily Jun–Sept 1, 10am–6pm. Closing times vary. $31.75 adults, $23 children (ages 4-9).

Wild Water's 100 acres teem with water slides, wave pools, a river float, and a Caribbean Cove, a mega-pool complete with waterfalls and a rock-climbing wall. For little tykes, the Dolphin Bay playground is the place to be.

Out-of-Town Musts For Kids

Ready for a road trip? These kid-friendly excursions outside the city are well worth the drive.

African Lion Safari★

1386 Cooper Rd. in Cambridge, 32km/20mi northwest of Hamilton by Hwy. 8, right on Rte. 552 north after Rockton and left on Safari Rd. 519-623-2620. www.lionsafari.com. Open Jul–Labour Day daily 10am–5:30pm. Late Apr–Jun & rest of Sept–mid-Oct daily 10am–4pm. $22.95 adults, $16.95 children (ages 3–12).

Kids, you'll need your parents to drive the family car (or you can ride the safari tram for an added cost) through the various enclosures of African and North American free-roaming animals. But watch out—at the monkey jungle, a horde of African baboons will climb all over your car and try to steal any removable part they can!

Clifton Hill

Leads from River Road on the Niagara Parkway to intersect with Victoria Avenue.

A tourist promenade that has been likened to Las Vegas for its colourful signage and over the top properties like Ripley's Believe It Or Not museum and the Guinness World Record Wax Museum, this steep street overlooks Niagara Falls and is the hub of wax museums, shops, and restaurants. Over 35 attractions call Clifton Hill home. The kids will enjoy visits to the Cosmic Coaster Ride, Dinosaur Park, and the ferris wheel ride called the Skywheel as parents pop over for miniature golf and to Movieland.

Marineland Niagara Falls

7657 Portage Rd., Niagara Falls. 209km/130mi southwest of Toronto. Take the Gardiner Expwy. West to Queen Elizabeth Way (QEW). Follow QEW to Niagara Falls and take Exit 30 and Rte. 420 to downtown. 905-356-9565. www.marinelandcanada.com. Open daily May 18-June 18 10am-5pm; June 18-Aug 31 9am-6pm; Sept 1-Oct 12 10am-5pm. $37 adults, $30 children (ages 5–9).

Get ready for views of beluga whales and killer whales along with shows that take place above and below the water, you have an opportunity to feed and touch these friendly ocean giants in specially scheduled sessions. Sea lions and dolphins are also on hand. When you tire of marine creatures, the park features about a dozen rides including a carousel, a roller coaster and a Ferris wheel.

Bird Kingdom in Niagara Falls

5651 River Road in Niagara Falls. 866-994-0090 and 905-356-8888. www.niagarafallsaviary.com. Open daily July-Aug 9:30am-7pm. Sept 10am-5pm (Sat until 7pm). Oct-Feb 10am-5pm. $14.95 adults; $9.95 youth (5-12).

On the former site of the Niagara Falls Museum, this aviary which opened in 2002 is a virtual bird kingdom housing birds as well as slithery reptiles and tropical fish. Children can get up close to view macaws at the Macaw Market, catch a glimpse of bats at the nocturnal zone or just hang out at the small or main aviary. Daily programs include bird shows, educational sessions and personal encounters.

Canada's Wonderland

9580 Jane St., Vaughan. 30km/19mi north of Toronto via Hwy. 400 and Rutherford Rd. 905-832-7000. www2.cedarfair.com/canadaswonderland. Open late May–mid Oct Nov daily 10am. Closing times vary. $56.20 rides passport; $30.99 grounds.

Plan to spend a good part of the day at Canada's first themed park. The outdoor wave pool can keep you happy for hours, but there are over 200 games, rides, restaurants and shops to wile away the hours. Take the time to climb the man-made mountain and experience the various rides and shows. Be sure to visit Kidzville and Nickelodeon Central, which has Dora the Explorer among other familiar cartoon characters.

Ready for some fun? From high tea to the high seas, there's certainly a lot of fun in Ontario's capital.

Ice-skating at Harbourfront Centre★★

On Queens Quay W., south of York Quay Centre. 416-973-4866. www.harbourfrontcentre.com. $7 adults, $6 children. Rink open in winter daily 10am–10pm, weather permitting.

Winter offers the opportunity for outdoor ice-skating. Overlooking the harbour, the Natrël Rink at Harbourfront Centre has skaters glide across the ice to music. There's even an indoor changing room. Bring your own skates or rent a pair here.

The Waterfront★★

235 Queen's Quay W. 416-973-4000. www.harbourfrontcentre.com.

The area south of Front Street is home to such modern landmarks as CN Tower and the Rogers Centre. At the water's edge, several quays house colourful shops, galleries, performance spaces, restaurants and an outdoor stage known as **Sirius Satellite Radio Stage**. Most of all, it's a great place to experience the breezes and sparkle of Lake Ontario.

Cruising

Cruises depart May-Sept daily from the docks around Harbourfront Centre, 235 Queen's Quay W. 416-973-4000. For schedules and fares, contact individual companies or check online at www.harbourfrontcentre.com.

One of the best ways to appreciate Toronto's glittering skyline is from the water. In the warmer months *(generally May-Sept)*, a variety of cruises are available from a two-hour harbour tour to an all-day charter and shipboard dinner and dancing. Vessels range from Canada's largest sailing ship, the Tall Ship *Empire Sandy (416-364-3244; www.empiresandy.com)* to three-masted Great Lakes schooners *(416-260-6355; www.greatlakesschooner.com)* and tour boats with enclosed decks.

Hippo Tours

151 Front St. W. 416-703-4476 or 877-635-5510. www.torontohippotours.com. Tours May–Nov 1 daily every hour on the hour from 11am-6pm. $38 adults, $25 children.

This brightly coloured 40-seat amphibious "bus that floats" takes passengers on a 90-minute, narrated, land-and-water tour past attractions such as the CN Tower and the Flatiron Building then over to Ontario Place for a cruise inside the breakwater.

Hockey Hall of Fame★

At Brookfield Place (formerly BCE Place,)
30 Yonge St. 416-360-7765. www.hhof.com.
Mon-Fri 10am-5pm. Sat 9:30am-6pm;
Sun 10:30am-5pm. $13

If hockey's your game, you can experience
all aspects of the sport at the Hall of Fame.

NHLPA Be A Player Zone – Experience a
virtual face-off with Wayne Gretzky and
Mark Messier in this expanded "faux-ice"
rink. You can watch your points rack up on
the multimedia scoreboard.

TSN/RDS Broadcast Zone – If you've
always wanted to be a hockey broad-
caster, now's your chance to narrate the
play-by-play action on the Be A Player
Zone rink. Just remember, it's your call!

Pepsi Game Time – Think you know
hockey? Test your skills with over 8,000
hockey questions at this multimedia
competition.

Hockey—The Real Thing

For hockey action, the Toronto Maple Leafs' season runs mid-Sept to early
April *(home games at 7:30pm)*. Tickets may be difficult to come by—hockey
being the national pastime—but try Ticketmaster *(416-872-5000, www.ticket-
master.ca)* or the Air Canada Centre, their home turf *(416-815-5500; www.
theaircanadacentre.com)*. Otherwise, show up at the box office at Air Canada
Centre *(40 Bay St. near Lake Shore Blvd.)* the morning of the game (be there at
9am) to get a wristband. When you return that evening, you just might get in.

Catch a Baseball Game

Join local fans at the Roger Centre *(see Landmarks)* for Toronto Blue Jays' action *(season runs Mar–Sept)*. The two-time World Series champions square off with opposing American League teams most weeknights at 7:05pm for home games *(Sat 1:05pm, Sun 4:05pm; check www.torontobluejays.com for current schedule)*. Get your tickets online or call the Toronto Blue Jays Information line *(416-341-1111)* or Ticketmaster *(416-872-5000, www.ticketmaster.ca)*.

Tea Treats

When in Toronto, enjoy a classical tea break in the afternoon. A number of big hotels serve high tea about 2:30pm. Your choice of premium loose-leaf tea comes complete with all the traditional accompaniments: finger sandwiches, scones with clotted cream, pastries and petit fours. Here are some of the most elegant places for tea *(call for hours & prices)*:

Windsor Arms – *18 St. Thomas St. 416-971-9666. www.windsorarmshotel.com.*

Le Royal Meridien King Edward Hotel – *37 King St. E. 416-863-9700. www.lemeridien/kingedward.*

The Fairmont Royal York – *100 Front St. W. 416-368-2511. www.fairmont.com.*

Yonge Dundas Square

On the southeast corner of Yonge St. and Dundas St. 416-979-9960. www.ydsquare.ca

In the heart of downtown Toronto across from the bustling shopping emporium of the Eaton Centre, the new Yonge Dundas Square promises to entertain in this public open space entertainment venue. When city planners green lit this urban project, it was because the intersection of Yonge and Dundas, considered Toronto's number one visitor destination, badly needed a make-over

Cooking Schools and Demonstrations

Chef wanna-be's and foodies, grab your apron for these cooking demos and classes-they're fun *and* delicious!

Bonnie Stern School of Cooking
6 Erskine Ave. 416-484-4810. www.bonniestern.com.

Local cookbook author Bonnie Stern offers three-hour demonstrations with seasonal themes like spring celebration and grilling and barbecues. Stern could prepare 8-10 recipes per class.

Great Cooks and The T Spot
The HBC, 401 Bay St. on floor 8. 416-861-4727. www.greatcooks.ca.

Chefs from Toronto's top restaurants teach classes here that combine demonstrations with do-it-yourself methods using a wide range of menus from around the world.

Dish Cooking Studio
390 Dupont St., 2 blocks west of Spadina. 416-920-5559. www.dishcookingstudio.com.

Hands-on and demo classes with top chefs focus on international cuisine. Some programs even offer field trips—perhaps an Indian Spice Tour or a walk through Chinatown—in addition to cooking instruction and dinner.

Calphalon Culinary Center
425 King St. W. 416-847-2212 or 877-946-2665. www.calphalonculinarycenter.com.

In the trendy King West district, a former factory warehouse now houses Toronto's newest cooking school. Chefs-in-the-making watch a demo class like a live cooking show or get hands-on at their own cooking station.

with its then garish discount shops. Now surrounded by huge animated billboards showcasing the newest movies along with monster-sized marquees of the latest advertising campaigns, visitors can easily feel the overt commercialism here. At the same time, festivals, concerts along with sights of up and coming performers, frequently take place here. In summer, by day it's *Summer Seranades* for the lunch-time music crowd, and by night, it's *Global Grooves*, a free concert series celebrating world music. You can even pick up discount tickets at the T.O. Tix discount ticket booth located here. On the weekends, artisan markets are popular. Events are planned throughout the year at this renovated site that officially opened in 2003.

Recreational Trails

Ranked as the No. 1 cycling city in North America, Toronto has over 840km/ 522mi of trails. Try t**he Highland Creek Trail** *(Northern Dancer Blvd. to Don Roadway in the east)* or the 22km/14mi Martin Goodman Trail along the waterfront. So grab your bike, put on your walking shoes or step into a pair of in-line skates and have some fun while you exercise.

For details about the city's trails, contact Toronto Parks & Recreation: 416-392-8186 or www.city.toronto.on.ca/parks.

Beltline Trail occupies a former railway. The 3.3km/2mi trail begins at the old train bridge crossing over Yonge Street at Mount Pleasant Cemetery and ends west of Bathurst. Tree-lined most of the way, the trail is ideal for a summer jog or cycle.

The **Boardwalk** in the city's east end neighbourhood, The Beach, runs about 3km/1.8mi along the shores of Lake Ontario. The wide-planked wooden walkway edges the sand and leads to Ashbridge's Bay Park, where walking paths continue along the waterfront. It's not usual to see joggers out on the Boardwalk as early at 6am and as late as midnight.

The **Don Trail** starts at the corner of Lakeshore Boulevard and Don Roadway, and then travels all the way north to Edwards Gardens at Lawrence Avenue East. This trail system consists mainly of paved, off-road paths lining the river, with some sections heading through parks.

Highland Creek Trail, in the eastern part of the city, begins at the intersection of Kingston Road and Celeste Drive and follows the banks of Highland Creek for an estimated 6km/3.7mi out to the natural shoreline of Lake Ontario. The city's most secluded trail, it cuts through a deep, lush valley and several parks.

Martin Goodman Trail, Toronto's contribution to the Waterfront Trail *(below)*, runs about 20km/12mi along Lakeshore Boulevard, from the Beaches east of downtown to Humber Bay Park, west of the city core. With a few exceptions, this off-road trail is paved; it's especially popular because it's flat for most of the route. One section does take cyclists on bike lanes on city streets, including traffic-clogged Queen's Quay East.

The **Toronto Islands** are paved with vehicle-free roads along their entire length, from City Centre Airport to Ward's Island, passing beaches (including one that's clothing-optional) along the way. Some ferries have restrictions on bikes, so it's best to check in advance.

Waterfront Trail *(www.waterfronttrail.org)* stretches more than 200km/ 124mi along the shores of Lake Ontario from Stoney Creek *(75km/47mi south-east of Hamilton)* to Quinte West *(161km/100mi east of Toronto)*. The trail takes cyclists, walkers and in-line skaters though and past towns such as Oakville, Mississauga and Port Hope. Parks along the way have picnic tables and toilets. When completed, the trail will extend a total of 650km/403mi, from Niagara to Gananoque.

As the third-largest theatre centre in the English-speaking world (after London and New York City), Toronto keeps audiences entertained with a wealth of performances ranging from Broadway musicals to cabaret and dinner theatre.

Roy Thomson Hall★★

60 Simcoe St. at King St. 416-593-4822, Ext. 385. www.roythomson.com. Roy Thomson Hall box office also handles tickets for Massey Hall and the Toronto Symphony.

Resembling a large, inverted glass-sheathed bowl, Roy Thomson Hall is home to the Toronto Symphony Orchestra and the Toronto Mendelssohn Choir. A thick circular passageway creates a "sound lock" around the performance area, assuring the hall's superior acoustics *(see Landmarks for the hall's history).*

Elgin and Winter Garden Theatre★

189 Yonge St. 416-314-2901. www.heritagefdn.on.ca.

This splendid structure, which re-opened in 1989 after an extensive renovation, contains the world's last remaining double-decker theatre. The 1,500-seat Elgin, with its ornate box seats, and the 1,000-seat Winter Garden, characterized by its fanciful ceiling of hanging beech boughs, opened in 1913 and 1914 as vaudeville houses. Today the theatres host a variety of mainstream shows, plays and concerts.

Air Canada Centre

40 Bay St. 416-815-5500; 416-872-5000. www.theaircanadacentre.com. Behind-the-scenes tours available: 416-815-5982.

This state-of-the-art 665,000sq ft sports and entertainment complex can seat 19,800 fans to see top-name performers like Britney Spears, U2 and the Rolling Stones. Home court for the Maple Leafs (NHL), the Raptors (NBA) and the Toronto Rock lacrosse (NLL) teams, Air Canada Centre also presents shows such as Sesame Street Live and Disney on Ice.

Canon Theatre

744 Victoria St. 416-364-4100. www.mirvish.com.

With over 3,300 seats, the Canon ranked as Canada's largest and most lavish theatre when it opened in 1920. Located in the heart of downtown, the Canon mainly accommodates touring Broadway musicals.

Short On Cash?

For same-day, half-price tickets visit the **T.O. Tixs** booth *(southeast corner of Dundas Square, at Dundas & Yonge Sts.)* on the day of the performance. *For a daily list of half-price shows, call 416-536-6468, Ext. 40*. T.O. Tixs is also a Ticketmaster Canada and TicketKing outlet.

Four Seasons Centre for the Performing Arts

145 Queen St. W. 416-363-8231 or 800-250-4653. www.fourseasonscentre.ca.
Building tours are available most Saturday mornings at 11:45am and 12 pm. Adults $7.

Bounded by University Ave., Queen, Richmond and York resides Toronto's new home to the Canadian Opera Company and the National Ballet of Canada. Designed by Toronto architect Jack Diamond, the 2,000 seat theatre is considered the first building of its kind in Canada designed for opera and dance. The seats and acoustics of this five-storey horseshoe-shaped amphitheatre allow for the best possible sight lines and the finest sound quality.

As the majority of seating occurs around the orchestra level, escalators are not found. For seating in the upper levels, you can use a brilliant floating stairwell, which is the world's longest freespan glass staircase, or one of three large elevators. Besides the scheduled performances by the two companies, you can also register for building tours or enjoy a free concert series in the Richard Bradshaw Amphitheatre.

Factory Theatre

125 Bathurst St. 416-504-9971. www.factorytheatre.ca.

Founded in 1970, the Factory devotes itself exclusively to presenting Canadian plays. Housed in a Victorian mansion an eclectic mix of Canadian productions including many ground-breaking new works are on stage.

Sony Centre for the Performing Arts

1 Front St. E. 416-393-7469 or 416-872-2262.
www.sonycentre.ca

The former homes to the National Ballet of Canada and to the Canadian Opera Company, the centre continues to present a program of Broadway musicals, comedy, lectures,

concerts and family shows. Designed by Canadian modernist architect Peter Dickinson, the centre originally known as the O'Keefe Centre opened in 1960 with Richard Burton and Julie Andrews starring in *Camelot*.

Lorraine Kimsa Theatre for Young People

165 Front St. E. 416-862-2222. www.lktyp.ca.

This stage produces productions for youth and focuses on works by Canadian playwrights.

Massey Hall

178 Victoria St. 416-872-4255. www.masseyhall.com.

Music of all genres have delighted audiences at this landmark 1894 concert hall. After you attend a performance in the 2,753-seat amphitheatre, enjoy a drink at Centuries Bar & Lounge downstairs, teeming with portraits and playbills dating back to the hall's first concert.

All This, And A Meal, Too

If you want to dine *during* the performance, check out these dinner theatres.

Famous People Players Dinner Theatre *110 Sudbury St. 416-532-1137 or 888-453-3385. www.fpp.org. Closed Sun & Mon.* Life-size puppets are brought to life musically by performers who are developmentally challenged. Dinner is a three-course sit down affair.

Mysteriously Yours Dinner Theatre *2026 Yonge St. 416-486-7469; 800-668-3323. www.mysteriouslyyours.com.* Dine while you help solve an on-stage whodunit.

Stage West All Suite Hotel & Theatre Restaurant *5400 Dixie Rd. 905-238-0159 or 800-668-9887. www.stagewest.com.* This cabaret-style buffet-dinner theatre hosts plays, concerts and tribute shows with internationally known stars.

Princess of Wales Theatre

300 King St. W. 416-872-1212 or 800-461-3333 www.mirvish.com.

This 2,000-seat playhouse opened in 1993 in the core of the Entertainment District. Its stunning interior is decked out with Venetian terrazzo floors, blown-glass lamps, mahogany panelling and 10,000sq ft of murals by artist Frank Stella. Long-running award-winning musicals such as Disney's *The Lion King* performed here.

Royal Alexandra Theatre

260 King St. W. 800-724-6420. www.mirvish.com.

A national historical monument dating to 1907, the "Royal Alex" boasts an honor-roll of great performers including John Gielgud, Helen Hayes, Orson Welles and Humphrey Bogart. Long-running shows like *MAMMA MIA!* have been on stage in its sumptuous interior.

St. Lawrence Centre for the Arts

27 Front St. E. 416-366-1656. www.stlc.com.

The centre houses the Bluma Appel and Jane Mallett theatres, which present productions performed by StLC's six resident companies: CanStage, Music Toronto, Toronto Operetta Theatre, Opera in Concert, Esprit Orchestra and Hannaford Street Silver Band.

What's Up?

Check Toronto's official online guide to theatre, dance and opera, **www.goliveTO.ca** is the source to learn about the latest entertainment events. For information about what's playing where in Toronto, pick up a free copy of *Now* or *Eye Weekly* magazine, or check online at: *www.totix.ca.*

Second City Toronto

56 Blue Jays Way. 416-341-0011.
www.secondcity.com.

Improv, and sketch comedy are the
focus of the Second City troupe.
This Toronto stage has seen the start
of many A-list comedians. Famous
alumni include John Belushi, Dan
Aykroyd, John Candy, and Mike Myers.

Tarragon Theatre

30 Bridgeman Ave. 416-531-1827. www.tarragontheatre.com.

Started in 1970, the Tarragon carries on its mission to "develop, encourage and
produce new work." Major playwrights whose work premiered here include
David French, Joan MacLeod, and Judith Thompson. On Sunday matinees,
ticket prices are offered as "pay-what-you-can."

Theatre Passe Muraille

16 Ryerson Ave. 416-504-7529.
www.passemuraille.on.ca.

Housed in a former bakery
factory, Passe Muraille specializes in alternative theatre.
Pay-what-you-can prices are
available for previews and
Sunday matinees.

Toronto Centre for the Arts

5040 Yonge St., North York. 416-733-9388. www.tocentre.com.

Toronto Centre in North York showcases a wide range of music, theatre and
dance. Performances occur at the Main Stage Theatre, the George West Recital
Hall, and Studio Theatre.

Tickets, Please

In general, you can purchase tickets at individual theatre box offices or through
Ticket Master Canada *(416-870-8000; www.ticketmaster.ca).*

TicketKing *(416-872-1212 or 800-461-3333)* handles ticket sales for the Royal
Alexander Theatre, the Princess of Wales Theatre and the Canon Theatre.

You don't have to pass an art-appreciation course to enjoy Toronto's diverse and eclectic canvas of galleries, which feature everything from contemporary glass to early Inuit art. Here's a sampling of some of the more high-profile properties.

Jane Corkin Gallery

The Distillery, 55 Mill St., Bldg 61. 416-979-1980. www.corkingallery.com.

Jane Corkin has an established reputation for showcasing fine vintage, modern and contemporary photographs and has her collection housed in the Distillery District, the former Gooderham and Worts distillery. *(see Historic Sites).*

Mira Godard Gallery

22 Hazelton Ave. 416-964-8197. www.godardgallery.com.

One of Canada's largest commercial art galleries boasts three floors of exhibition space containing paintings, sculptures and limited-edition photographic prints by Canadian and international artists.

Odon Wagner Gallery

196 Davenport Rd. and 172 Davenport Rd.
416-962-0438. www.odonwagnergallery.com.

Odon Wagner offers two galleries in tony Yorkville. View modern and contemporary paintings at the new 172 Davenport location. At the flagship gallery opened since 1969, it's historic art specializing in 18C and 19C European paintings.

Sandra Ainsley Gallery

The Distillery, 55 Mill St., Bldg. 32; 416-214-9490. www.sandraainsleygallery.com.

Specializing in glass and mixed media, Sandra Ainsley features N. American and international artists like Hiroshi Yamano, Richard Whiteley and Tania Lyons.

Yorkville Galleries

The Yorkville area, particularly along Yorkville and Hazelton Avenues, offers a mix of galleries within a short stroll of each other. **Maslak Mcleod Gallery** *(118 Scollard St.; 416-944-2577; www.maslakmcleod.com)* specializes in North American Aboriginal art including paintings, sculptures and catalogue exhibitions. Try **Miriam Shiell Fine Art Ltd.** *(16-A Hazelton Ave.; 416-925-2461; www.miriamshiell.com)* for international modern and 20C contemporary works of art. **Ingram Gallery** *(49 Avenue Rd. at Yorkville Ave.; 416-929-2220; www.ingramgallery. com)* represents upcoming and known contemporary artists from across Canada. Other good galleries to peruse are Gallery Gevik *(12 Hazelton Ave.; 416-968-0901; www.gevik.com)* and Kinsman Robinson Galleries *(108 Cumberland St.; 416-964-2374; www.kinsmanrobinson.com).*

Whether your fashion tastes run to haute couture or vintage clothing, you can do serious damage to your credit card in Toronto's shopping areas.

Eaton Centre★

220 Yonge St. between Queen St.W & Dundas St. W. 416-598-8560. www.torontoeatoncentre.com.

This five-level office/shopping mega-structure boasts 285 retail stores and eateries. Retailers include Sears, Pottery Barn, Old Navy, Godiva Chocolatier and Laura Secord, Canada's premier chocolate maker since 1913 (a visit to Bally Total Fitness or Good Life Fitness may be in order afterwards!). Stores like Limite, Urban Planet, Aritzia and Jean Machine appeal to Gen-Xers, while sports enthusiasts flock to Sport Chek. Food courts offer a wide range of dining-on-the-go options.

Shopping Underground

Neither rain nor snow nor sleet will deter the truly determined shopper, but Toronto's 27km/16mi-long subterranean shopping plaza certainly makes shopping a lot more pleasant. Beneath the city's streets, **PATH** links 1,100 stores, shops and restaurants, 48 office towers and six hotels from Eaton Centre to Union Station. There are more than 125 street-level access points. When you're in the underground network, the letters in PATH act as guides. Each letter is a different color and indicates a different direction.

The Beach

Queen St. E.

This area is as packed with shops as it is with cars and people. Take the convenient Queen Street street car east to avoid the hassle of parking. A collection of one-of-a-kind shops blends with restaurants and big retail chains like The Body Shop, Starbucks and Pier 1 Imports. The best blocks for shopping are on Queen Street between Glen Manor Drive and Herbert Avenue.

Bloor/Yorkville and Hazelton Lanes

Between Yonge & Avenue Rd., 55-87 Avenue Rd.

For upscale shopping, head to the Bloor/Yorkville neighbourhood *(Bloor St. between Bay & Avenue Rd. and Cumberland & Yorkville Sts.)* and the tony Hazelton Lanes shopping mall *(Yorkville & Hazelton Sts.; 416-968-8600; www. hazeltonlanes.com)*. This is where you'll find Whole Foods Market, high-end boutiques like Gucci, Hermès, and Prada. Think of it as Toronto's Rodeo Drive.

Danforth Avenue

Between Broadview & Pape Aves. www.thedanforth.ca

If you're looking for fashion and accoutrements for the home, come to trendy Danforth Avenue, where you'll find stores such as Design by Asia, and Elan. Parking is difficult, especially on warm summer evenings when patrons spill out of the restaurants onto the many sidewalk cafes.

Hudson's Bay Company (HBC)

176 Yonge St. 416-861-9111. www.hbc.com.

First chartered in 1670 by King Charles II, the Hudson's Bay Company had exclusive trading rights to some 40 percent of the lands in Canada. Today it lives on, in a chain of department stores. From Eaton Centre you can reach "The Bay" by a covered walkway across Queen Street.

Kensington Market

West of Spadina Ave., north of Queen St.W. www.kensington-market.ca

For vintage clothing, the best place to shop is Kensington Market, a multicultural neighborhood best known for fishmongers, cheese shops, spice stores, delis, and of course, used garment shops.

Second-hand clothing outlets like Courage My Love *(14 Kensington Ave.),* Vintage Depot *(70 Kensington Ave.)* and Planet Aid *(160 Baldwin St.)* draw repeat patrons.

Queen Street West

East of Spadina Ave.

Mainstream brand stores like Gap, Club Monaco and Zara have arrived to this once avante-garde location that used to appeal to the hipster crowd. For edgier fashions, you need to head farther west *(Queen St. west of Bathurst St.)*, where hip designers stock one-of-a-kind rags. Look for an eclectic collection of shops and kitschy names, like 69 Vintage, for new clothes re-fashioned from old, and Heel Boy for designer shoes.

Desperately Seeking Antiques

Antique hunters will find a smattering of stores along **Mount Pleasant Avenue** *(between Soudan & Millwood Sts.)* and along **Queen Street East** *(between Leslie & Carlaw Sts.).* The new **Toronto Antique Centre** *(276 King St. W.; open Tue–Sun; 416-345-9941; www.torontoantiquectr.com)* offers over two dozen stalls packed with antiques and collectibles. It's easy to find, sandwiched between the Royal Alexandra and Princess of Wales theatres.

Queen's Quay Terminal

207 Queen's Quay W. 416-203-0510. www.toronto.com.

For shopping near Lake Ontario, Queen's Quay offers about 30 shops, selling everything from jewellery to home accessories. First Hand, Proud and Arctic Nunavut specialize in Canadian-crafted products; Oh Yes, Toronto (sic), stocks souvenirs emblazoned with the city's name. There's a food court on the second level, plus three lakeside restaurants, two with outdoor patios.

Suburban Malls

From Club Monaco to the Disney Store, you can fulfill all your shopping needs in the two levels of the newly expanded **Fairview Mall** that recently under-went an $84-million renovation *(Hwy. 404 & Sheppard Ave. E.; 416-490-0151; www.fairviewmall.ca).* Here you'll find over 270 shops and services including a new Fairview Food Garden seating 700 patrons. **Yorkdale Mall** too completed a $60-million expansion, and now *(3401 Dufferin St., adjacent to Hwy. 401; 416-789-3261; www.yorkdale.com)* has over 240 retailers, anchored by The Bay also known as HBC and Sears. Thirteen full-service restaurants give shoppers a chance to sit down and refuel.

If you like to party well into the wee hours, check out College Strip (Little Italy), Danforth Avenue (Greektown), Queen Street West and Yorkville for lively restaurants, hot clubs and relaxing lounges. Overall, you'll find the greatest concentration of clubs in the Entertainment District *(the blocks between John, Duncan and Peter Sts. running north and south; and Queen, Richmond and Adelaide Sts. running east and west)*. Here are some of the hottest places to mix, mingle, dine and dance until 2am (when bars stop serving alcohol)—or later.

The Drake Hotel

1150 Queen St. W., 416-531-5042. www.thedrakehotel.ca.

Once a seedy dive the historic hotel in Toronto's trendy West Queen West Art and Design District is now reborn as a chic cosmopolitan crash pad attracting

hipsters and trend setters who arrive to socialize. The party really starts a-going when the crowds usher into one of the hotel's three favourite hang-outs. At the Lounge, you sit back in the plush banquettes and sip their classic cocktails like La Floriditas and Mai-Tais. At the Underground Bar, turn your groove on and get freaky. The place thrives on the indie-music scene. On starry nights head up to the rooftop patio for more music and for great views of the hood.

Ba ba lúu

136 Yorkville Ave. 416-515-0587. www.babaluu.com.

Considered the neighbourhood of the well-heeled, Yorkville offers a number of clubs including this longtime Latin hot spot. This popular supper club serves tapas and a limited menu of entrées. Dancing to salsa music continues until 2:30am. Learn the moves on Sunday night with a free salsa lesson.

The Fifth Social Club

225 Richmond St. W. 416-979-3000. www.TheFifth.com.

With its alley entrance and old-fashioned freight elevator, The Fifth has that prohibition feel as it's housed in a multilevel warehouse. Expect a polished crowd of young professionals for drinks and dancing *($10 cover)*.

Fluid Lounge

217 Richmond St. W. 416-593-6116.

For dancing under high-tech laser lighting, try the Fluid Lounge. This let-loose kind of place caters to an upscale set with two dance floors and a mix of funk, industrial, house and hip-hop.

Lula Lounge

1585 Dundas St. W., west of Dufferin. 416-588-0307. www.lulalounge.ca.

Sounds of Cuba and the latest Spanish rhythms come alive at this nightclub. There's no formality here. Folks can sit back, sip a signature mojito, order from the Latin fusion menu or hit the dance floor. Salsa lessons are taught by a Cuban choreographer most Fridays and every Saturday.

Li'ly

656 College St. 416-532-0419. www.lilylounge.com

This hot spot has a clubby atmosphere, albeit one that caters to the 20-something set with reasonable drink prices for the College Street area. Billed as a "boutique bar," Li'ly serves an international tapas menu and 40 different martinis. Bars on two separate levels don't start jumping until after 10pm.

Myth

417 Danforth Ave. 416-461-8383. www.myth.to

This local favourite, which serves Mediterranean cuisine in a smart-casual setting *(see Must Eat)*, welcomes a party crowd around 10pm. People tend to drop in here before heading to other clubs. On Friday and Saturday evenings a DJ spins tunes from 10pm to 3am.

Roof Lounge

*18th floor of the Park Hyatt, Bloor St. & Avenue Rd. 416-324-1568.
www.parktoronto.hyatt.com.*

Enjoy upscale light fare in this elegant rooftop lounge as you overlook the new ROM with its cascading crystal-feel. The food is presented in innovative vessels such as Bento boxes and Cuban cigar boxes. Steaks, pastas and salads are also available.

The Melody Bar

1214 Queen St. W., The Gladstone Hotel. 416-531-4635. www.gladstonehotel.com.

Situated in an intimate lounge with an original 30s bar, you think you're in another era, with décor is accented by high ceilings, and columns. This bar, which is part of The Gladstone Hotel, serves up nightly music and is the city's karaoke hub.

Panorama Lounge

51st floor of the Manulife Centre, 55 Bloor St. W. 416-967-0000.

One of the city's best views of the downtown core can be had here. Relax outside under the stars on one of two patios, sip martinis or choose from a menu of 50 other cocktails.

Souz Dal

636 College St. 416-537-1883.

Behind its rather rusty looking exterior, Souz Dal is a dark, intimate martini bar featuring a menu with some 60 cocktails, including three dozen flavoured martinis. A late-night cocktail in the tiny back room, open to the stars during the summer season, will enhance any romantic evening.

Wine Lovers

Crush Wine Bar

455 King St. W. 416-977-1234. www.crushwinebar.com

This sleek fine-dining restaurant has an extensive wine list, plus an eclectic selection of wines by the glass. Sip a chilled Reisling on the courtyard patio.

Far Niente

187 Bay St. 416-214-9922. www.farnientegrill.com.

Far Niente's lower-level wine bar is filled with blond woods and wine racks. Selections are from the award-winning-and fairly priced-wine list.

Sneaky Dee's

431 College St. 416-603-3090. www.sneaky-dees.com.

This fixture on the corner of Bathurst and College is hard-to-miss. Its brightly coloured sign resembling grafitti is a sure clue that things are rockin' inside. No wonder locals call it Sneaky's. With a concert hall upstairs and restaurant on the main floor, here's where you can put back a few pints and listen to the blues.

Reds Bistro & Bar

77 Adelaide St. W. First Canadian Place. 416-862-7337. www.redsbistro.com.

Catering to the Financial District crowd, sophisticated Reds offers some 80 wines by the glass on its acclaimed wine list. The place picks up from 5pm–8pm weekdays, when the business crowd drops by for Happy Hour.

All That Jazz

Cover charges vary for the clubs listed below, depending on the night and who's performing. For more information on jazz in Toronto, check online at: www.jazzintoronto.com.

Rex Jazz & Blues Bar

194 Queen St. W. 416-598-2475. www.therex.ca

A hotel since the 1950s, the Rex is not fancy, but the place has been a gathering place for jazz lovers since the late 1980s. If you're in town during the annual Downtown Jazz Festival, you just might catch big names like Harry Connick Jr. jamming on this stage.

Horseshoe Tavern

368 Queen St. W. 416-598-4753. www.horseshoetavern.com.

This legendary bar in business since 1947 continues to showcase musicians and has been the stepping stone for many great bands. Famous alumni who performed lately include The Tragically Hip, Blue Rodeo, and Hootie & The Blowfish. When The Police released their debut album in 1978, they also hopped on this stage making their Toronto debut. The Horseshoe is still rocking and continues to book breaking bands. A recent make-over adding new floors, and new chairs and tables, has also put a new face on the Old Lady.

After a rough day of shopping or sightseeing, treat yourself to a trip to one of Toronto's professional day spas. Those listed below offer a full menu of services, including hair care—some even serve lunch, or at least fresh fruit and tea.

Elizabeth Milan Hotel Day Spa

At The Fairmont Royal York, 100 Front St. W., Arcade level. 416-350-7500. www.fairmont.ca.

Professional treatments and services are the order of the day within this serene, Mediterranean-themed space, where the pace is deliberately slow. Skin care is a specialty and the Swedish massages are particularly heavenly. Jennifer Lopez, Sarah Ferguson and other celebrities have been pampered here.

The Elmwood Spa

18 Elm St. 416-977-6751. www.elmwoodspa.com.

The multilevel Elmwood specializes in aesthetics and massages. Water therapies take place in the spa whirlpool, as well as in the swimming pool, sauna and steam room. At lunchtime, treat yourself to Thai-influenced cuisine on the pool deck in the comfort of your spa robe and slippers.

Holtz Spa

At the Hilton Suites, 8500 Warden Ave., Markham. 905-470-8500. www.holtzspa.ca.

A body-cocooning waterbed and a futuristic-looking aromatherapy capsule available for a variety of body treatments are two spa novelties found at this sleek, high-tech urban spa. On the cutting edge of spa treatments, Holtz offers a Swiss shower complete with steam and multi-coloured lighting.

Old Mill Inn Spa

At the Old Mill Inn & Spa, 21 Old Mill Road. 416-232-3700. www.oldmilltoronto.com/spa.

Scents of lavender, rosemary and mint permeate many of the treatments at this busy hotel spa from the Tudor Rose Body Wrap to a personalized aroma-therapy massage. The staff's attention to the tiniest of details ensures that you will be pampered from head massage to toe manicure.

Stillwater Spa

At the Park Hyatt, 4 Avenue Rd. 416-926-2389. www.stillwaterspa.com.

With its trickling water features, fireplaces and special lighting, Stillwater instantly creates a sense of calm and serenity when you arrive. Popular treatments include aqua therapy, Zen shiatsu massage and the Honey Body Glow. On Saturday after-noons, special treats are passed around the tea lounge on silver trays.

The Spa at Windsor Arms

8 St. Thomas St. 416-971-9666. www.windsorarmshotel.com.

With just seven treatment rooms, The Spa is as intimate and exclusive as the Windsor Arms itself. One unique treatment is Tui Na, a deep-muscle massage mixing Chinese and shiatsu techniques. The adjacent swimming pool area is a one-of-a-kind haven for relaxation: where else would you find a pool with a fireplace? Tranquility prevails throughout.

Victoria Spa

In the International Hotel, 225 Front St. W., 3rd floor.
416-413-9100. www.victoriaspa.com.

Newly relocated to the International Hotel, Victoria Spa ushers patrons into a calm-inducing space accented with Asian artifacts. Offerings include a full range of aesthetics and therapeutic massages for men and women, plus a juice bar. Take a dip in the sparkling indoor pool or sun yourself on the outside deck under the looming CN Tower.

Votre Beauté European Day Spa

At the Westin Harbour Castle, One Harbour Square. 416-203-8483.
www.votrebeautespa.ca.

High-end contemporary Italian décor, a floor-to-ceiling waterfall and original art create an upscale environment for a full range of body therapies here. A few of the more popular treatments are the 144-jet hydro tub, a waterfall shower and an organic apple body polish.

Spa Getaways

Although they're located about an hour's drive from Toronto, these spa resorts are nonetheless well worth the trip and they offer overnight accommodations and meals.

High Fields Country Inn & Spa

11568-70 Concession 3, RR#1, in Zephyr. 905-473-6132 or 888-809-9992.
www.highfields.com.

An hour north of Toronto, High Fields commands a hilltop overlooking Ontario's farm-lands. Horse pastures, and walking paths surround the rambling inn. New-age treatments such as chakra-balancing and Japanese reiki are offered along with traditional treatments. Try the signature Himalayan rejuvenation treatment, or a hot-stone massage.

The Hillcrest of Valenova Inn & Spa

175 Dorset St. W. 905-885-7367 or 888-253-0065. www.thehillcrest.ca.

Tucked away on 14 wooded acres in residential Port Hope, about an hour east of Toronto, The Hillcrest welcomes guests to its grand mansion. Among the amenities are an outdoor pool, fitness room, sauna, and gourmet cuisine. Choose from a full complement of treat-ments, including facials, manicures, pedicures, hydrotherapy, massag-es, wraps and exercise sessions. Try the ancient Hawaiian massage or the Golden Moor Mud facial.

Toronto is diverse enough to offer something for just about everyone. But if you want a break from the big city, Toronto's enviable location makes it easy to access other sights along the Lake Ontario shoreline, as well as places to the north. These must-see excursions lie within a two-hour drive of Toronto.

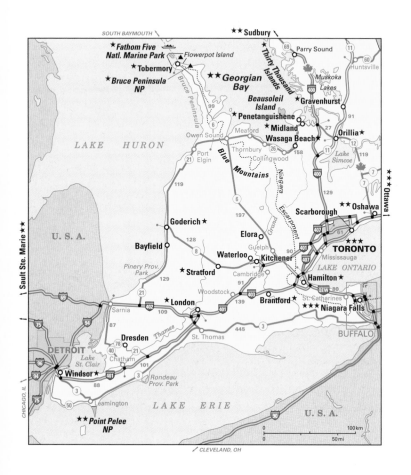

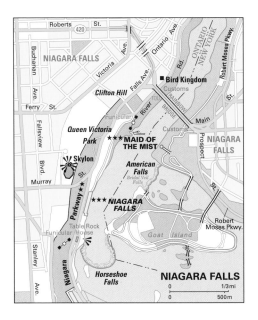

Niagara Falls★★★

209km/130mi southwest of Toronto. Take the Gardiner Expwy. West to Queen Elizabeth Way (QEW). Follow QEW to Niagara Falls. Take Exit 30 and Rte. 420 to downtown. 905-356-6061 or 800-563-2577. www.niagarafalls.com.

Southwest of Toronto, the natural and man-made attractions of Niagara Falls are as popular as ever. In the 19C Niagara was a hucksters' paradise where every conceivable ruse was used to separate tourists from their money. The Province of Ontario and the State of New York stepped in, buying all the land on both sides of the river adjacent to the falls. Today green parks line the riverbank and visitors can enjoy the natural beauty.

You can see **The Falls**★★★ from the riverbank level, from the water level at the bottom of the cataract, or from the top of various towers constructed especially for viewing purposes.

Maid of the Mist★★★

Access from River Rd. Elevator at foot of Clifton Hill. 905-358-0311. www.maidofthemist. com. Departs from Maid of the Mist Plaza late May–Labour Day daily 9am; Apr–mid-May and rest of Sept–late Oct daily 9:45am. Closing hours vary. $14. Elevator & boat ride operate weather permitting.

Even though you're provided with a hooded raincoat for this trip, you'll still get wet on this exciting half-hour boat ride . After passing the American Falls, the boat goes to the foot of the horseshoe cataract, the best spot to appreciate the water's mighty force .

Best View of Niagara Falls ★★★

5200 Robinson St. 905-356-2651. www.skylon.com. Open Jun–Labour Day daily 8am–midnight. Rest of the year daily 10am–10pm. $12.

For a spectacular view of the falls board the elevator at the **Skylon Tower.** Known as yellow bugs go up to the observation deck, which rises 236m/775ft above the falls.

Niagara River Facts

Length: Approximately 56km/35mi
Starting Point: Lake Erie
Ending Point: Lake Ontario
Flow: South to north
Speed: Approximately 64km/40mi per hour
Horseshoe Falls: 52m/170ft in height
American Falls: 55m/180ft in height

Walk from Rainbow Bridge to Table Rock ★★★

Rainbow Bridge at River Rd. 877-642-7275. www.niagaraparks.com. Tunnels open mid-May–Labour Day daily 9am–9pm (Fri, Sat, Sun until 11pm). Rest of the year, call for hours. Closed Dec 25. $7.50.

Begin this 1.6km/1mi walk at Rainbow Bridge. Stroll south passing **Queen Victoria Park** and its beautiful flower beds. Continue to Table Rock, where it's possible to stand on the brink of Horseshoe Falls on the Canadian side. Watching the water thunder over the edge is an awesome experience.

In Table Rock House, descend by elevator to start your Journey Behind the Falls tour. Walk this catacomb of tunnels to see the immense curtain of falling water.

Leave The Driving To The People Mover

There's no need to drive once you've arrived at the falls. In summer, you can park at the Rapids View lot ($6.50/car); the rest of the year there's parking at the Falls lot ($12/car; 877-642-7275; www.niagaraparks.com). Then hop aboard the People Mover, which stops at more than 20 attractions along **Niagara Parkway** between the falls and Queenston Heights Park. Shuttle buses run every 20min mid-Jun–early Sept daily 9am–11pm; rest of Sept–late Oct daily 10am–6pm *(Sat until 10pm)*. Get your tickets at the main terminal *(7369 Niagara Pkwy.)*; in summer you can also buy tickets at the People Mover booths located along the parkway *($7.50; unlimited boarding throughout the day)*.

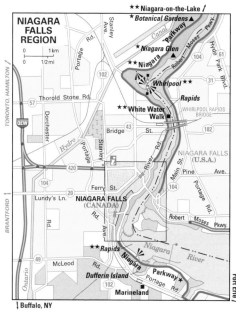

Niagara Parks Botanical Gardens★

2565 Niagara Pkwy. 877-642-7275. www.niagaraparks.com. Open year-round daily dawn–dusk. Closed Dec 25. Free. Parking $12.

Students at the Niagara Parks Commission School of Horticulture maintain the beautiful 32ha/80-acre gardens. The **rose garden** is particularly lovely in early June.

Niagara-on-the-Lake★★

21km/13mi north of Niagara Falls via the Niagara Pkwy. North . 905-468-1950. www.niagaraonthelake.com.

Known as one of the prettiest towns in Canada, and indeed it is; you'll feel like you're in an English village here. Settled by Loyalists (those loyal to the British king during the American Revolution), the town was the first capital of Upper Canada (Ontario). Burned to the ground by the Americans during the War of 1812, it was rebuilt and seems to have changed little since. Today Niagara-on-the-Lake has a delightful collection of shops, restaurants, galleries and lovely homes. It's also home of the **Shaw Festival**, an eight-month-long celebration of plays by Irish playwright George Bernard Shaw (1856–1950) and his contemporaries.

Queen Street★ – Niagara-on-the-Lake's wide main thoroughfare centres on a handsome clock tower.

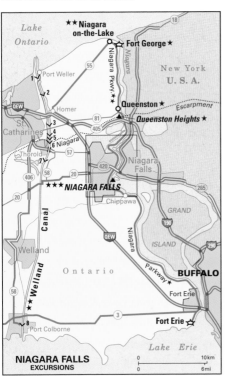

NIAGARA FALLS
EXCURSIONS

Niagara Apothecary – *5 Queen St. 905-468-3845. Open May–Labour Day Mon-Fri noon–6pm, weekends 10am–6pm. Rest of Sept–mid-Oct weekends only 10am–6pm. www.niagara-apothecary.ca.* In this 1866 pharmacy, you can see an array of wares and instruments used in the 19C trade.

Shaw Festival Theatre – *Queen's Parade & Wellington St.* This brick structure with a beautiful wood interior serves as the main theatre for the festival. Performances are held from April to November *(Tue–Sun noon, 2pm & 8pm; for information, call 800-511-7429 or visit www.shawfest. com).*

Fort George★ – *26 Queen St., near the Shaw Theatre. 905-468-6614. Open May 1 - Nov 30 daily 10am–5pm. Rest of the year by appointment. $11.* Built by the British in the 1790s, this fort played a key role in the War of 1812, being alternately captured by the Americans and recaptured by the British. Visit its grassy earthworks and a wooden palisade enclosing officers' quarters, forge, powder magazine, guardhouse and blockhouses.

Oshawa★★

58km/36mi east of Toronto. Take the Gardiner Expwy. East to the junction of Kingston Rd. Continue east to the junction of Hwy. 401 and take Exit 417 into Oshawa. 905-725-4523 or 800-667-4292. www.oshawa.ca/tourism.

East of Toronto, on the north shore of Lake Ontario, sits the industrial city of Oshawa. One of the main centres of Canada's automobile industry, its name has long been synonymous with industrialist and philanthropist Robert S. McLaughlin, whose former home is open to the public.

Parkwood Estate★★

270 Simcoe St. N., 4km/2.5mi north of Hwy. 401. 905-433-4311. www.parkwoodestate.com. Open Jun–Sept Tue–Sun 10:30am–4pm. Rest of the year Tue–Sun 1:30pm–4pm. Closed major holidays. $7.

At this imposing 55-room residence, built by Robert S. McLaughlin in 1917, you can see how the immensely wealthy McLaughlin family lived. The house contains priceless antiques, and every room displays furnishings of the finest woods and fabrics. Be sure to wander in the beautiful 5ha/12-acre **gardens**; then stop at the pleasant **teahouse** set beside a long reflecting pool *(in summer, light lunch and afternoon tea are served Tue–Sun 11am–4pm).*

Canadian Automotive Museum ★

*99 Simcoe St. S., about 1.5km/1mi north of Hwy. 401. 905-576-1222.
www.oshawa.ca/tourism/can_mus. Open year-round Mon–Fri 9am–5pm,
weekends 10am–6pm. Closed Dec 25. $5.*

Inside the former McLaughlin
manufacturing plant learn the
history of Canada's automobile
industry. Among the collection
you'll find about 65 automobiles
in mint condition, mostly from
1898 to 1981.

Robert McLaughlin Gallery

*72 Queen St. in the Civic Centre next to city hall. 905-576-3000. www.rmg.on.ca.
Open year-round Mon–Fri 10am–5pm (Thu until 9pm), weekends noon–4pm.
Closed Jan 1, Jun 30, Aug 4 & Dec 25. Admission by donation.*

Originally built in 1969, the expanded gallery designed by Arthur Erickson
displays the works of the Painters Eleven, a group of artists who united in the
1950s to exhibit abstract art in Toronto. Changing exhibits feature contemporary Canadian art.

Robert McLaughlin

Apprenticed at his father's carriage works for three years, Ontario native Robert
Samuel McLaughlin (1871–1972) converted the business into a motor company. He
started making auto bodies in 1908 for the Buick company, located in the US, in
Michigan. In what was to become his famous McLaughlin Buick *(above)*, he used an
American engine. He sold the company in 1918 to the General Motors Corp., but
remained chairman of the Canadian division, whose main plant is in Oshawa. Less than
10 years later, the Oshawa plant, employing 3,000 people, was manufacturing more
vehicles than the rest of the country combined.

Best Excursions From Toronto

Hamilton★

113km/70mi west of Toronto via Queen Elizabeth Way. 905-546-2666 or 800-263-8590. www.tourismhamilton.com.

West of Toronto lies Hamilton. This former steel centre is known for its botanical gardens and historic sites. The modern downtown along Main Street contains several attractive buildings—in particular City Hall, the Education Centre, the **Art Gallery★**, and Hamilton Place (a cultural centre with two theatres). A few blocks west stands **Hess Village★** *(Hess & George Sts.),* a collection of older homes that have been transformed into funky and fashionable boutiques, restaurants and cafes.

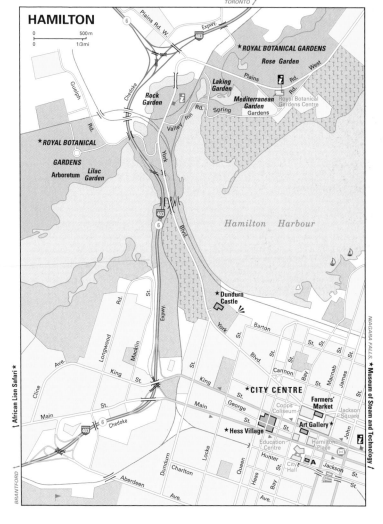

Sir Allan

Sir Allan Napier MacNab was a member of the Family Compact, a group of wealthy men with strong British ties who dominated the government of York—and Upper Canada—in the 1830s. His castle illustrates the wealth and power of the group's members.

In 1838 Queen Victoria knighted him for fighting against William Lyon Mackenzie *(see Historic Sites)*, and in the 1850s, he served two years as prime minister of Canada when it was a province. Despite living in such a big house and having many servants, MacNab died in debt.

Dundurn Castle★

610 York Blvd. 905-546-2872. www.hamilton.ca. Visit by guided tour only, July–Labour Day daily 10am–4pm. Rest of the year Tue–Sun noon–4pm. Closed Jan 1 & Dec 25–26. $10.

This grand stone house stands on a hill overlooking Hamilton Bay. A showplace of 19C privilege, the residence was completed in 1835 and belonged to Sir Allan Napier MacNab, prime minister of the Province of Canada from 1854 to 1856. Step inside to see the elaborately furnished interior. On the grounds outside is a small military museum *(open 11am–5pm; included in castle admission fee)*.

Museum of Steam and Technology★

900 Woodward Ave., just south of Queen Elizabeth Way. 905-546-4797. Open Jun–Labour Day Tue–Sun 11am–4pm. Rest of the year Tue–Sun noon–4pm. Closed major holidays. $6.

Hamilton's former water-pumping station, completed in 1859, now provides a rare example of 19C steam technology. With its arches and cast-iron columns, the engine house contains two Gartshore steam-powered beam engines of 1859. They pumped as many as five million gallons of water a day until they were replaced in 1910. The old boiler house features displays on the use of steam power and a working model of the beam engines.

Royal Botanical Gardens★

680 Plains Rd. W. 905-527-1158. www.rbg.ca. RBG Centre open year-round daily 9am–dusk. Gardens open Apr–Oct daily 9:30am–dusk; rest of the year daily 9:30am–6pm. Closed Jan 1 & Dec 25. $10. Free shuttle bus Apr–Oct.

These diverse gardens stretch over 1,000ha/2,700 acres of land at the western tip of Lake Ontario. Much of this area is natural parkland with walking trails. Several featured gardens are worth visiting.

Mediterranean Garden – *At the Royal Botanical Gardens Centre (RBG Centre).* This conservatory houses vegetation from the five regions of the world with a Mediterranean climate (the Mediterranean Rim, Southern Africa, Australia, California and Chile).

Laking Garden – *Just west of RBG Centre.* This garden abounds in irises and peonies *(May–Jun)* and herbaceous perennials *(May–Oct).*

Rose Garden – *In Hendrie Park, across the road from RBG Centre.* The rose garden features magnificent displays *(May–Oct)* of some 2,000 hybrids and 650 shrub roses. Be sure to see the climbing variety as well as low-maintenance plantings.

Rock Garden – *York Blvd., west of Laking Garden.* A whirl of color in summer, the rock garden features flowering plants and shrubs set in the midst of water and rocks.

The Arboretum – *Old Guelph Rd., northwest of Rock Garden.* Growing within the arboretum, the lilac garden is a fragrant feast for the senses when the bushes bloom in late May to early June.

Wasaga Beach★

138km/86mi north of Toronto via Hwy. 401 west to Hwy 400 north to Barrie. Take Rte. 26 north to Rte. 27 north, then west at Elmvale on Rte. 92. 705-429-2247 or 866-292-7242. www.wasagainfo.com.

In warmer weather, Ontarians head to the world's longest freshwater beach around Nottawasaga Bay well known for its 14km/9mi stretch of white sand beach and its water parks.

Beach Area One

Beach Dr.

This beach is where the action is—particularly for the young. Try your hand at beach volleyball or just relax on the sand. Other diversions include miniature golf, shopping, or eating at one of the many restaurants nearby.

Wasaga Beach Provincial Park

Beach Dr., between Beach Area One & Two. 705-429-2516. www.ontarioparks. com. Open late Jun–Labour Day Mon–Fri 9am–10pm, weekends 8am–10pm. Rest of the year, call for hours.

Especially favoured by families, this shoreline park boasts eight areas equipped with picnic tables and changing facilities with toilets. The shallow bay waters are a boon for kids. If you're seeking quiet, the extreme western areas are usually less crowded.

Wasaga Waterworld

Main Park at River Rd. W. (Hwy. 92) & Theme Park Rd. Second location at Beach Area One. 705-429-4400 or 800-809-0896. www.wasagawaterworld.com. Open late Jun–Labour Day daily 10am–6pm. $24/day pass.

Take your pick of the speed and serpent slides or grab a tube to ride the Giant Wave Pool. There's also a heated whirlpool, a children's pool and colorful bumper-boat rides. When you get tired of the water, you can play miniature golf or visit the arcade.

Wasaga 500

152 River Rd. W. (Hwy. 92), 2mi east of Wasaga Beach. 705-322-2594. Open Jun– Aug daily 10am–11pm; call for off-season hours. $4/one lap, $20/7 laps.

Before the 1970s, people were allowed to drive their cars on the sand at Wasaga Beach. Now, wearing a seat belt and a safety helmet, you can steer a go-kart around a 1mi asphalt track—and not get sandy.

Must Stay: Hotels

The properties listed below were selected for their ambience, location and/or value for money. Prices reflect the average cost for a standard double room for two people (not including applicable taxes). Hotels in Toronto often offer special discount rates on weekends and off-season. Properties are located in Toronto, unless otherwise specified. Quoted rates exclude the taxes for GST, PST and DMF which equal a total of 13%. For a complete listing of hotels mentioned in this guide, see Index.

Luxury	**$$$$$** over $300	**Moderate**	**$$$**	$125–$200
Expensive	**$$$$** $200–$300	**Inexpensive**	**$$/$**	$75–$125/under $75

Luxury

The Hazelton Hotel
$$$$$ 77 rooms

118 Yorkville Avenue, at the NW corner of Hazelton and Yorkville Aves. 416-963-6300 or 866-473-6301. www.thehazeltonhotel.com

In the heart of swanky Yorkville amid the chi-chi shops stands the new nine-story luxe Hazelton Hotel. Toronto's first small leading hotel of the world is big on glam and does not disappoint. A condo-hotel, guests have access to the five-star hotel located from floors two through four. The suites are 40s Hollywood chic with a nod to modern luxuries such as plasma televisions, Tivoli clocks and sumptuous leather sofas. Expect to find nine-foot high walls with floor to ceiling windows that gives the perfect perch from which to view the hustling Yorkville scene below. Use the complimentary hotel limousine service to downtown. Pamper yourself to the full-service spa and fitness centre with lap pool. Book the high-tech screening room for private film showings. The hotel's restaurant One is helmed by celebrity chef Mark McEwan whose specialty is haute Canadian cuisine.

Le Royal Meridien King Edward
$$$$$ 298 rooms

37 King St. E. 416-863-9700 or 800-543-4300. www.toronto.lemeridien.com.

The "King Eddie," as it's locally known, dates to 1903 and the reign of King Edward VII. Marble pillars, a vaulted ceiling, and fine period pieces now characterize Toronto's first completely fireproof hotel. A grand piano graces the sizable

lobby, which provides easy access to hotel shops and services. Edwardian guest rooms are fit for a king, with mahogany furnishings, elegant window treatments and marble baths. Crowned by a baroque plasterwork ceiling, the airy, palm-studded **Café Victoria ($$$)** makes a lovely spot for a meal.

Soho Metropolitan $$$$$ 92 rooms
318 Wellington St. W. 416-599-8800 or 866-764-6638. www.sohomet.com.

Located in the downtown entertainment district, this luxury boutique hotel is just steps from the lively nightlife. Rooms offer avant-garde design and décor, and high-end amenities like Frette linens, European down duvets and heated marble floors. It's also home to **Senses ($$$)** restaurant and bakery, which serves globally inspired cuisine.

Sutton Place $$$$$ 294 rooms
955 Bay St. 416-924-9221 or 866-378-8866. www.suttonplace.com.

This stylish hotel in tony Yorkville is a favourite with visiting celebrities. Old World charm and discretion combine with modern-day comforts here. Marble floors, lush carpets, and antique furnishings adorn its European-style lobby. Spacious well-lit guest quarters contain traditional furnishings in dark or blond woods and feature full amenities for business travellers.

Windsor Arms $$$$$ 28 rooms
18 St. Thomas St. 416-971-9666 or 877-999-2767. www.windsorarmshotel.com.

Around the corner from bustling Bloor Street and neighbouring Yorkville, this boutique hotel revives a 1927 Gothic Revival structure, complete with a fortress-like entrance. Inside, luxury meets high technology in 26 suites (and two deluxe rooms) equipped with fireplaces, limestone baths and Jacuzzi tubs. The celebrated **Tea Room** becomes a champagne and caviar bar nightly, and the hip, newly renotaved bar 22 features cocktails. In the **Courtyard Café ($$$$)**, posh surroundings and impeccable service complement superb continental cuisine.

Expensive

The Fairmont Royal York
$$$$ 1,365 rooms.

100 Front St. W. 416-368-2511 or 800-441-1414. www.fairmont.com.

Toronto's landmark is a palatial property. From its imposing lobby—complete with balconies and chandeliers—to its grand ballrooms, the hotel exudes an aura of majesty. Royalty, not to mention countless celebrities, have made the Royal York their home away from home. Guest rooms are outfitted with buttery yellow walls, elegant window treatments and period reproduction furnishings. **Epic ($$$)** wins raves for its French cuisine.

Hotel Le Germain Toronto
$$$$ 122 rooms

30 Mercer St. 416-345-9500 or 866-345-9501. www.germaintoronto.com.

Sleek, clean and contemporary are the words that leap to mind when considering the décor of this upscale boutique hotel. Entertainment-district restaurants, theatres and clubs are an easy stroll away, as is the Rogers Centre and CN Tower. On-site facilities include a work-out room, a massage room and a rooftop terrace.

Metropolitan
$$$$ 426 rooms

108 Chestnut St. 416-977-5000 or 800-668-6600. www.metropolitan.com.

Asian influences permeate this swank downtown hotel. An open two-storey lobby welcomes guests with marble floors, wood trim and gleaming brass railings. Contemporary accommodations sport blond woods, glass and neutral color schemes. The award-winning **Lai Wah Heen ($$$)** restaurant, whose name means "luxurious meeting place," serves some of the best Cantonese fare in the city.

The Old Mill Inn & Spa
$$$$ 60 rooms

21 Old Mill Rd. 416-232-3707 or 866-653-6455. www.oldmilltoronto.com.

Overlooking the Humber River, this secluded hotel avoids big city bustle, but is near upscale Bloor West Village for shopping. Handsomely furnished guest rooms include a fireplace and whirlpool tub; most rooms have river views. Pamper yourself at the on-site spa *(see Spas)* before dining and dancing to a live band *(Mon–Sat)* in the inn's restaurant. Rates include a complimentary breakfast.

Moderate

Gloucester Square Inn of Toronto
$$$ 25 rooms

512-514 Jarvis St. 416-966-3074 or 800-259-5474. www.gloucestersquare.com.

A few blocks from Church Street Village (Toronto's gay community), this inviting inn offers lodging in two restored Victorian houses. Cheerful decorated rooms have four-poster and cast-iron beds and ceiling fans; most have private baths and terraces. Afternoon tea is included, or try the 24-hr room service.

Grand Hotel & Suite Toronto $$$ 177 rooms
225 Jarvis St. 416-863-9000 or 877-324-7263. www.grandhoteltoronto.com.

This all-suite hotel includes complimentary breakfast and in-room high-speed Internet access in the room rate. The amenities include a rooftop patio with two Jacuzzis, fitness centre, massage room and meeting space.

Hotel Victoria $$$ 56 rooms
56 Yonge St. 416-363-1666 or 800-363-8228. www.hotelvictoria-toronto.com.

Near shops, restaurants and attractions like the Hockey Hall of Fame, this small boutique hotel offers compact standard rooms that are stylishly decorated in dark woods and peach and grey tones. Deluxe rooms have ironing boards, mini-fridges, coffeemakers and baths with above-counter vessels. Rates include a continental breakfast.

Madison Manor Boutique Hotel $$$ 23 rooms
20 Madison Ave. 416-922-5579 or 877-561-7048. www.madisonavenuepub.com.

This lovingly restored Victorian mansion is set in the Spadina Avenue/Bloor Street area. Guests here enjoy antique-furnished, individually decorated rooms. The hotel is a five-minute cab ride to the theatre district and other downtown attractions.

Strathcona Hotel $$$ 194 rooms
60 York St. 416-363-3321 or 800-268-8304. www.thestrathconahotel.com.

Situated around the corner from Union Station, right in the middle of the Financial District, the Strathcona has a pleasant lobby facing busy York Street. Recently refurbished rooms may be on the small side, but are cheery and comfortable. In-room amenities include hair dryers, coffeemakers and ironing boards; corporate rooms are equipped with data ports and dual-line phones. For an extra $10, guests can use the nearby fitness club.

Suite Toronto $$$ 100 rooms
372 Richmond St. W. 416-595-5599 or 866-867-8483. www.suitetoronto.com.

This property provides furnished suites in various new condo apartments located near CN Tower, Rogers Centree, Air Canada Centre and the shops and theatres of the Entertainment District. All condos boast extras like a fully equipped kitchen, laundry facilities, 27-inch TV, DVD and stereo system and high-speed Internet access.

Town Inn Suites $$$ 200 rooms
620 Church St. 416-964-3311. www.towninn.com.

Town Inn offers a range of condo-style suites, all comfortably appointed with separate living and sleeping areas. Located within walking distance of the Bloor and Yonge Street shops and restaurants, the inn features exercise options in an indoor heated pool, a sauna and a weight room.

Inexpensive

Alexandra Apartment Hotel
$$ 78 rooms

77 Ryerson Ave. 416-504-2121 or 800-567-1893. www.alexandrahotel.com.

Situated at the quiet end of a residential street close to a park, the Alexandra contains all studio suites with kitchenettes. Coin-operated laundry facilities are available on most floors. It's a 20-minute walk to downtown attractions, and the public library and the community centre with its pool are just steps away.

Banting House Inn Bed & Breakfast
$$ 7 rooms

73 Homewood Ave. 416-924-1458. www.bantinghouse.com.

Bordering Cabbagetown, this classic Edwardian heritage home features bedrooms mostly with shared baths. Themed rooms have names like Oriental Room, Wedgewood Room, and the Oscar Wilde Room, with its private bath and balcony. There's $10 parking in a gated driveway and an Asian-inspired backyard garden.

Beaches Bed & Breakfast
$$ 4 rooms

174 Waverley Rd. 416-699-0818. www.members.tripod.com/beachesbb/.

Located in The Beach near shops, restaurants and the lakeside boardwalk, this private home holds eclectically decorated guest quarters (check out the Jungle theme). Rooms have private or shared bathrooms and telephones. Two rooms have kitchenettes and a balcony or garden terrace. Internet access is available for the asking.

Bonnevue Manor Bed & Breakfast by the Lake
$$ 3 rooms

33 Beaty Ave. 416-536-1455. www.bonnevuemanor.com.

This heritage home is walking distance to the city's Eastern European community. Generous-size rooms are bright, nicely decorated and have private baths. The Martin Goodman Trail and High Park lie nearby.

The Residence College Hotel
$$ 420 rooms

90 Gerrard St. W. 416-351-1010.

A former nurses' residence, this high rise adjacent to Toronto Hospital maintains clean, modest rooms (only 30 of which are double) with single beds, desks and telephones. Bathrooms are shared, European-style. Guests have use of the communal TV lounge, fully equipped kitchen and laundry facilities on each of 15 floors. The best feature is the glassed-in health club with its full-size swimming pool, two squash courts and weight room—all free to hotel guests.

The Toronto Townhouse $$ 6-8 rooms

213 Carlton St. 416-323-8898 or 877-500-0466. www.torontotownhouse.com.

A Cabbagetown heritage home, Toronto Townhouse offers six to eight rooms (depending on the time of year) with either private or shared facilities. The largest room has a king-size bed and sitting area; another room has a kitchenette. Breakfast is served in the open kitchen overlooking the garden.

Global Village Backpackers $ 196 beds

460 King St. W. 416-703-8540. www.globalbackpackers.com.

Located in the King and Spadina area, this no-frills hostel contains both private and shared rooms. Guests have access to self-catering facilities, a coin-operated laundry and Internet service. You'll be within walking distance of CN Tower, SkyDome, the shops and restaurants of Queen Street West and the King Street Entertainment District.

The venues listed below were selected for their ambience, location and/or value for money. Rates indicate the average cost of an appetizer, entrée and dessert for one person (not including tax, gratuity or beverages). Most restaurants are open daily and accept major credit cards. Call for information regarding reservations, dress code and opening hours. Restaurants listed are located in Toronto unless otherwise noted. For a complete listing of restaurants mentioned in this guide, see Index.

Luxury	$$$$	over $50
Moderate	$$$	$35–$50
Budget	$$/$	$20–$35/less than $20

Luxury

Canoe $$$$ Canadian

66 Wellington St. W. 416-364-0054. www.oliverbonacini.com.

Overlooking the harbour and the Toronto Islands from its perch on the 54th floor of the Toronto Dominion Bank Tower, this perennial hot spot caters to a professional crowd by combining haute Canadian cuisine with excellent service. Signature dishes include Alberta red deer loin, roast Arctic char, and Maritime lobster salad. Minimalist décor mixes country pine and polished concrete to create a cool but comfortable setting.

The Fifth $$$$ French

225 Richmond St. W. 416-979-3005. www.thefifth.com.

A monthly changing fixed-price, five-course menu satisfies diners in this elegant and intimate dining room. Here you'll be greeted by skirted chairs, white linens, a fireplace and live piano music. A different menu (but one that's just as tasty) is served on The Terrace, a rooftop patio.

Splendido

$$$$ International

88 Harbord St. 416-929-7788. www.splendido.ca.

This Annex neighbourhood restaurant offers a unique selection of fresh Canadian ingredients with Mediterranean accents. Old and New World wines complement dishes like chilled Ontario green asparagus soup with Dungeness crab, Alberta beef steak tartar, and seared Alaskan halibut Provençale. For dessert, you'll be tempted by the Tahitian vanilla-bean crème brûlée or a selection of domestic and imported cheeses served with Niagara dried fruits and walnut bread.

360, The Restaurant at the CN Tower

$$$$ Canadian Regional

In CN Tower, 301 Front St. W. 416-362-5411. www.cntower.ca.

The world's tallest revolving restaurant wins awards for its cuisine and wine list. Expect seared Atlantic salmon with risotto; mustard-crusted rack of lamb on olive smashed potatoes; or a three-tiered platter of Canadian seafood.

Moderate

Sassafraz
$$$ California-French

100 Cumberland St. 416-964-2222. www.sassafraz.ca.

Anchoring one of Yorkville's prime corners *(Cumberland & Bellair Sts.)*, this trendy eatery is a great spot for celebrity sightings (think Mick Jagger, Glenn Close, Denzel Washington). For lunch, a bistro menu—mussels, Croque-Monsieur, Niçoise salad—is available on the sidewalk patio facing busy Cumberland Street. Inside, the sunny yellow garden room blooms year-round with trees under a 12m/40ft atrium. Here you'll dine on the likes of purple-rice-crusted Atlantic salmon with chipotle beurre blanc, and medallion of veal tenderloin with white-truffle-scented potato gratin. Don't miss the lively jazz brunch on weekends.

Southern Accent
$$$ Cajun/Creole

595 Markham St. Dinner only. 416-536-3211. www.southernaccent.com.

Housed in a former Victorian residence, this funky Mirvish Village restaurant attracts a mixed crowd to its outdoor patio and small, mood-lit rooms located on different levels. Immerse yourself in the Mardi Gras ambience—start your meal with a Creole martini, made with Cajun pepper vodka. The menu changes monthly but perennial favourites include Creole jambalaya and blackened chicken livers. (Everything is à la carte, including the side dishes and yummy corn bread.) If it's available, save room for the N'Awlins bread pudding with Wild Turkey bourbon sauce.

Toula
$$$ Northern Italian

In the Westin Harbour Castle, 1 Harbour Square. 416-777-2002. www.toularestaurant.com.

From this restaurant's 38th-floor perch, you get a fabulous view of Lake Ontario and the Toronto Islands. Appetizers and entrées with Northern Italian accents are served amid a contemporary Italian décor rich with dark-wood cabinetry and a hand-painted gold-leaf ceiling.

Budget

Kalendar Koffee House
$$ Indian

546 College St. 416-923-4138.

Enjoy a beverage on the sidewalk patio, while sitting at the bar, or at one of the tiny tables in this casual College Street hangout. Try one of the house specialties—scrolls, crêpes with a variety of fillings; or Nannettes, appetizer-size, oven-baked nan bread with a choice of toppings.

Le Papillon
$$ French

16 Church St. Closed Mon. 416-363-0838. www.lepapillon.ca.

One of the few crêperies in Toronto, this rustic specialty restaurant serves up French and Québécois fare on a quiet street close to Hummingbird Centre. Stucco walls and checkered tablecloths over white linen create a romantic scene. In addition to a wide selection of crêpes—20 varieties, not including dessert—main dishes include tortière (a Québécois meat pie baked with sea-soned pork, beef and veal), and steak au poivre. Le Papillon's famous onion soup, smothered with Emmenthal cheese and filled with chunks of bread, is a meal in itself.

Marché $$ Continental

42 Yonge St., BCE Place. 416-366-8986. www. mövenpickcanada.com.

This bustling, downtown European-style restaurant features separate stations such as a grill and rotisserie, a salad stand, a pasta section and a bakery for fresh-from-the-oven muf-fins, breads and croissants. Themed seating areas include a French bistro and a potter's cottage arranged amid trees and potted plants.

Myth $$ Mediterranean

417 Danforth Ave. 416-461-8383. www.myth.to.

One of myriad Greek-style restaurants in Greektown, Myth is an open, high-ceilinged eatery with video screens and pool tables. A Mediterranean-style menu is available inside or on the popular sidewalk patio. Most-ordered en-trées include creative dishes like balsamic-glazed octopus, grilled vegetables with goat cheese, and lamb burger with Kaseri cheese and mint aïoli. Wash down a piece of sweet baklava with a cup of strong Turkish coffee for dessert.

The Red Tomato $$ International

321 King St. W. Happy hour & dinner only. 416-971-6626. www.redtomato.com.

Located in the King Street entertainment district, this cozy lower-level eatery (its higher-priced sister, **Fred's Not Here**, resides upstairs) is a good choice for pre and post-theatre meals. Expect an eclectic menu that includes salads, gourmet pizza, and pasta. The small plates are popular with the Happy-Hour crowd, and the baked lobster and crab soup is a house specialty.

Rodney's Oyster House $$ Seafood

469 King St. W. 416-363-8105. www.rodneysoysterhouse.com.

Without a reservation here, you may be saying "Aw shucks" when you hear there's an hour's wait. Rodney's is renowned for serving up some of the best shellfish in the city. The house specialty is fresh Malpeque oysters presented on the half-shell with a wide choice of condiments, including homemade pepper sauces. A meal at Rodney's is a night of boisterous, good old Maritime fun.

Pappas Grill $ Greek

440 Danforth Ave. 416-469-9595. www.pappasgrill.com.

One of the bustling Danforth neighbourhood's most popular restaurants, Pappas Grill is best known for clay-oven-baked pizzas and appetizers like Middle Eastern hummus and tzatziki dips. The diverse menu also offers plainer fare like burgers, pastas and salads.

Old Spaghetti Factory
$$ Italian

54 The Esplanade. 416-864-9761. www.oldspaghettifactory.com

A wide selection of pasta dishes here comes with sourdough bread, soup or salad, coffee and dessert. Tables set around a carousel and in and around a San Francisco trolley car create a fun ambience for kids. Good value.

Rainforest Café
$ American

Yorkdale Shopping Centre, 3401 Dufferin St. at Allen Pkwy. 416-780-4080. www.rainforestcafe.com

Located on the main level of the mall near the Famous Players Theatre entrance, the cafe re-creates a fanciful indoor rain forest complete with lush plants and cascading waterfalls. A varied menu offers appetizers, pizza, steak, seafood and pastas. Save room for the Volcano—a confection of brownies, ice cream, chocolate syrup and whipped cream.

East Side Mario's
$ Italian

151 Front St. W. 416-360-1917. www.eastsidemarios.com.

This spacious eatery features pasta dishes, roasted chicken and ribs, burgers, wraps, soups and salads. Kids will like the children's menu, which comes with a free ice cream and a free toy with each order.

Pickle Barrel
$ Eclectic

In Atrium on Bay, 312 Yonge St. 416-977-6677. www.picklebarrel.com.

The Pickle Barrel offers a fun atmosphere with a wide variety of menu items for picky young eaters. Expect selections like BBQ chicken and ribs, burgers, deli sandwiches, pastas, fajitas, salads and wraps. The 11 items on the children's menu include favourites such as grilled-cheese sandwiches and "chicken dinosaur nuggets."

Shopsy's
$ American

33 Yonge St. 416-365-3333. www.shopsys.com

A Toronto institution since 1921, this all-day dining spot is famous for its all-beef hot dogs and corned-beef sandwiches. Enjoy yours in indoor booths, on the spacious patio or as a to-go order from the busy take-out counter. There's a good range of sandwich platters, burgers and salads as well. Walls are lined with celebrity photos and caricatures.

Spring Rolls
$ Asian

693 Yonge St. 416-972-7655. www.springrolls.ca.

Sleek Asian décor and tasty, affordable Vietnamese, Chinese and Thai dishes attract students, a local office crowd and tourists to this two-level Yonge Street restaurant (there's a second location at 85 Front St. E.). Entrée specials change daily and include soup and salad. Pad Thai, Thai red curry, and stir-fries with Szechwan or black-bean sauce top the list of the most popular dishes. And don't forget the spring rolls!

Weekend Brunch

The Fairmont Royal York Hotel $$$

100 Front St. W. Sun 10am–2:30pm. 416-368-2511. www.fairmont.ca.

Epic, the Fairmont's signature restaurant, hosts this buffet brunch. Look for breakfast items, as well as seafood, a carving station, salads and even a sushi bar. The hotel offers free valet parking for the Sunday brunch crowd.

Le Royal Meridien King Edward Hotel $$$

37 King St. E. Sun 11am–3pm. 416-863-9700. www.lemeridien-kingedward.com.

A large selection of hot and cold dishes, including Beef Wellington, seafood, oysters, salads and pastries, is served buffet-style in the elegant **Café Victoria**.

Bloor Street Diner $$

55 Bloor St. W., in the Manulife Centre. Sun 11am–4pm. 416-928-3105. www.eatertainment.com.

This Bloor/Yonge Street area diner serves up seasonal salads, eggs made to order and roast beef. Be sure to visit the chocolate fountain for dessert.

Four Seasons Hotel $$

21 Avenue Rd. Sat & Sun 11:30am–2:30pm. 416-964-0411. www.fourseasons.com.

The **Studio Café** offers a fixed-price à la carte brunch with a selection of five starters, eight main courses and a choice of juice, coffee or tea.

Hot House Cafe $$

35 Church St. at the corner of Front St. Sun 9:30am–3pm. 416-366-7800. www.hothousecafe.com.

Live jazz and a buffet laden with staples like pancakes, eggs, salads and pasta make this a local favourite for brunch. Be ready to stand in line at the waffle and omelette stations.

Park Hyatt Hotel $$

4 Avenue Rd. Sat & Sun 11:30am–5pm. 416-925-1234. www.parktoronto.hyatt.com.

This classy Yorkville hotel offers an à la carte brunch menu in **Annona** restaurant. The menu is a combination of breakfast and lunch dishes *($14–$18 for appetizers; $17–$24 for entrées).*

Gallery Grill $

7 Hart House Circle. Closed Jul & Aug. Sun 11am–2pm. 416-978-2445. www.gallerygrill.com.

Located on the University of Toronto campus, the Gallery Grill offers an à la carte menu.

Irish Embassy Pub & Grill $

49 Yonge St. Sat & Sun 11am–3pm. 416-866-8282. www.irishembassypub.com.

A full Irish breakfast including pub fare like Irish stew and Kilkenny ale-battered haddock is offered here.

Lakefront Dining

Queen's Quay Terminal *(207 Queen's Quay W.)*, a retail/restaurant complex on the waterfront, has three restaurants overlooking the harbour: **Pearl Harbourfront Chinese Cuisine $$** *(on the second level; 416-203-1233)* specializes in Cantonese food; the **Boat House Bar & Grill $$** *(416-203-6300)* features pastas, pizza, steak, ribs, chicken and salads served indoors or on two patios with a view of Lake Ontario; **Il Fornello $$** *(416-861-1028)* serves up a variety of Italian specialties and offers the same great view.

Index

The following abbreviation may appear in this Index: PP Provincial Park.

Index

Index

Hotels

Nightlife

Bars/Clubs

Jazz Clubs

Shows

Index

Photos Courtesy Of

African Lion Safari: 74; Apa Publications/Richard Nowitz 3; Apa Publications/ Daniella Nowitz 16-17; The Bata Shoe Museum: 44-bottom; Black Creek Pioneer Village/©Rose Hasner/TRCA: 49-bottom, 71-bottom; Cadillac Fairview Corporation (unauthorized use not permitted.): 27; Campbell House 52; Gwen Cannon/ Michelin: 57-bottom, 66, 71-top, 76-top, 104-top, 104-bottom; City of Toronto – Culture Division: 9-middle, 55-top, 55-bottom, 56-top, 56-bottom, 58-top, 58-bottom; Courthouse Market Grill: 118-top, 118-bottom; Dee Dee Couch: icon 70-75; Dave Di Biase/SXC 37; The Distillery District/ ©photography Lucas Digital Art: 53; Elizabeth Milan Hotel Day Spa: 96; ©Fairmont Hotels and Resorts: 7-bottom, 38-top, 38-bottom, 39, 110-111, 116-117, 122; Le Royal Meridien: 122-bottom; Gardiner Museum of Ceramic Art: 45; Global Village Backpackers: 115; iStockphoto.com/Peter Spiro 18; iStockphoto.com/Vertex IS 21; iStockphoto.com/Eric Perelshtein 24; iStockphoto.com/ Andrew Chin 32; iStockphoto.com/Mary Marin 68; iStockphoto.com/Viktor Pryymachuk; Haldimand Hills Spa Village: 97-bottom; Harbourfront Centre: 72-top; Hummingbird Centre for the Performing Arts: 83; Andrej Kopac 92; Susan Law/www.osgoodehall.com; Le Royal Meridien: 122-bottom; Marvel Adventure City: 75-middle; McMichael Canadian Art Collection: 46; Metropolitan Hotel Toronto: 112; Mirvish Productions/ ©Ron Steinberg: 85-top; Mövenpick: 119; Odon Wagner Fine Art Gallery: 87; ©2003 Ontario Tourism: back cover, front cover – bottom left, 4-top, 4-middle, 4-bottom, 5-top, 5-bottom, 23, 29, 30-top, 42, 43, 57-top, 64, 73, 75-middle, 77-top, 77-bottom, 78, 82, 84-bottom, 90, 91, 92, 93, 95, 101, 103-top, 103-bottom, 106, 107, icon 98-109, 120; Paramount Canada's Wonderland: 75-bottom; Rouge Park: ©P. Money- 61, ©P. Brooks & D. Boileau- 62; ©Royal Ontario Museum, 2003. (All rights reserved.): 40-top, 40-bottom; 41-top, 41-bottom; icon 40-48; Second City – Stuart Broadcasting: front cover – bottom right, 86-top; Allison Simpson/Michelin: 5-middle, 5-bottom, 30-bottom, 31, 44-top, 60, icon 60-63, 94, 108, 113; Sony Centre 84-top; Splendido: 116-117, 117-bottom; Splendido and Chef David Lee icon 116-123; Theatre Passe Muraille: 86; Tommy Thompson Park: 63, 81; Toronto International Film Festival: 8-bottom; ©Toronto Public Library: 19, 20, 36, 59, 65-bottom; Toronto Reference Library: 35-top, 35-bottom; ©Toronto Tourism: front cover – top, 6-top, 6-middle, 7-top, 7-middle, 8-top, 8-middle, 9-top, 9-bottom, icon 22-39, 22-top, 22-bottom, 24, 25, 26, 28, 49-top, icon 49-59, 47, 50-top, 50-bottom, 51, 54, 65, icon 64-69, 67, 69, 72-bottom, 76-bottom, 79, 80, 88, 89; Victoria Spa: 97-top; Votre Beauté Spa: 97-middle.

Front cover – inside flap: base map ©Mapquest.com.
Apa Publications/Richard Nowitz: cover, front cover-top, front cover-left, front cover-bottom; Apa Publications/Daniella Nowitz: back cover.

Subway ~~Ossington~~ Kipling

go Port Credit

theloosemoose. ca